THE
BEATLES
APART

Titles in the
PROTEUS ROCKS
series include:

THE BEATLES APART
THE DAVID BOWIE PROFILE
KATE BUSH
ELVIS COSTELLO
LED ZEPPELIN 1968–1980
NEW WAVE EXPLOSION
THE POLICE
QUEEN
ROCK BOTTOM: THE BEST OF
    THE WORST IN ROCK
VISIONS OF ROCK
WHATEVER HAPPENED TO . . .?

PROTEUS BOOKS is an imprint of
The Proteus Publishing Group

United States
PROTEUS PUBLISHING CO., INC.
733 Third Avenue
New York, N.Y. 10017

United Kingdom
PROTEUS (PUBLISHING) LIMITED
Bremar House
Sale Place
London, W2 1PT

First published simultaneously
in the UK and US in 1981

Produced by
PILOT PRODUCTIONS LTD.,
London

Typeset by V & M Graphics Ltd, Aylesbury
Printed in Hong Kong by
Everbest Printing Co. Ltd.

ISBN: 0 906071 89 5

THE BEATLES
APART

Bob Woffinden

PROTEUS BOOKS
London and New York

CHAPTER

1

The Turning Point

The Beatles were at their apogee during 1967. That was the year which saw the release of *Sergeant Pepper's Lonely Hearts Club Band*, and in which they had performed 'All You Need Is Love' live before a world-wide audience of 300 million; well, not quite live, actually – George Martin had carefully prepared backing tapes – but few were going to quibble. The song was perfectly suited to the occasion: a universal message from the most universal artistes there had ever been.

In the wake of the release of *Sergeant Pepper* they had all taken a holiday, going to Greece. The album had been their most painstaking so far. Towards the end of August they returned to London, and with their wives (and, in Paul's case, girlfriend) went by train to North Wales for a Maharishi Mahesh Yogi weekend course. Cynthia Lennon didn't travel with the others; she had been unable to penetrate the police cordons at Euston station ("Mrs John Lennon? Yeah, that's what they all say, love") and had been driven up there independently by Neil Aspinall.

Though the accommodation was not as luxurious as they had become accustomed to, it was hardly ascetic, and the week-end had been developing promisingly when the Beatles received news of the death of Brian Epstein, and immediately took their leave of the Maharishi and, accompanied by a larger-than-ever posse of pressmen, returned to London.

The death was a great shock, but the Beatles reacted by announcing publicly that they would henceforth manage themselves. Further, they straightaway set to work – largely at Paul's instigation – on a new project, the *Magical Mystery Tour*. It was a sorry, shambling affair.

After the feeling of hubris undoubtedly generated by the overwhelming commercial and critical success of *Sergeant Pepper*, nemesis arrived with almost indecent despatch.

Although Epstein's death had been accidental, it was known that he had been becoming worried about what he felt to be his increasing redundancy. Having established

John's first wife, Cynthia, wipes a tear from her cheek as she is prevented by police from boarding the train in which the Beatles are travelling to Bangor to hear the Maharishi Yogi.

the group in Britain, in America, and throughout the world, and having rewritten all the rules of popular entertainment in doing so, it seemed as though the Beatles hardly needed a manager still. Although one can imagine him having felt like this, it could not have been further from the truth.

What instead happened was that after his death the Beatles were left without managerial guidance at precisely the moment when they were most in need of it – when overweening pride and a keen sense of infallibility had clearly laid pitfalls for the band.

Magical Mystery Tour was undertaken in just such an atmosphere. McCartney was determined to ensure that the group, though no longer touring (indeed, because they were no longer touring) should remain active, and should establish themselves as artistes *tout court*. In that hopelessly optimistic atmosphere, it didn't seem an impossible dream.

So they simply hired a coach, loaded it with forty-three passengers and unlimited stocks of colour film and set off for the West Country. Several of the forty-three seemed to have been chosen by dint of their physical extraordinariness, and included both the very small (a party of dwarves) and the very large (Jessie Robins, playing Ringo's outsize auntie). Just as the film's commentary suggested that the coach would gradually become immersed in magic on its journey, so no doubt the Beatles presumed that the mere selection of such a ragbag crew would ensure a ready supply of wondrous happenings. Certainly, they didn't try to pre-empt their muse by thinking up any of their own beforehand.

Hence the end result is just a succession of crudely-staged and generally unfunny sequences, presumably concocted in moments either of sublime self-confidence or of absolute desperation. Ringo, loyal as ever,

performed valiantly, but even he could not disguise the lack of script, structure and anything that could, even generously, be termed 'direction'.

The film was shown on BBC-TV on Boxing Day, and pricked the Beatles' bubble quite effectively. Within a few months of Epstein's death, they had already created problems for themselves, and blemished their hitherto perfect record sheet. It hardly helped the harmony within the group that the whole thing had been Paul's pigeon (and John cannily contributed as little as possible); especially since Paul had worked on the editing himself, and one couldn't help noticing that the visuals of himself that accompanied the 'Fool On The Hill' sequence seemed particularly narcissistic.

So, *Magical Mystery Tour* had showed the four of them working without the common purpose that had been evident all the while Brian Epstein had been managing them, and also, for the first time, floundering in their artistic endeavours. There were at this stage, however, no complaints about the music.

At the beginning of 1968, they recorded some fresh material for a new single. The choice was narrowed down to Paul's 'Lady Madonna' and John's 'Across The Universe', and when it fell on the former, John contributed his song to the World Wildlife Fund; one of its lines was paraphrased as the title of a compilation album, *No-One's Gonna Change Our World*. The B-side of 'Lady Madonna' was George's 'The Inner Light', which he had recorded in Bombay with classically-trained Indian musicians.

They all went to India early in the new year to complete their interrupted business with the Maharishi. Between bouts of meditation, they each prepared material for their next recording; from that point of view, their sojourn in India was a productive one.

By 1968, collaboration is effectively at an end

In most respects, however, the visit was hardly a success. Ringo left prematurely, offering his much-repeated quote that it was "just like Butlin's". Paul and Jane Asher, having arrived late, left early, to travel through India. John and George, the most ardent initiates, remained.

One Alexis Mardas was also with them there. A charismatic but somewhat disreputable Greek character, he made a big impact when he arrived on the Beatles' scene just before Yoko Ono. He preferred to be known by the soubriquet Magic Alex, and indeed John seemed to have believed that he had the ability to create magic. When Apple got under way, he was therefore placed in charge of the electronics division, in which capacity he sketched out blueprints for a hundred bizarre ideas, none of which he was able to put into practice, and managed to dissipate more of the Beatle fortunes than even the other divisions of Apple.

It was Magic Alex who relayed to John and George the news that the Maharishi had been doing what he ought not to have been doing with Mia Farrow, another of the celebrities present at the time. These allegations have never been substantiated, and it should certainly be borne in mind that they emanated from a less-than-reliable source. Nevertheless, both John and George became convinced of their veracity, and so they left India immediately, literally shaking the dust from their sandals with all possible haste. Subsequently, John wrote 'Sexy Sadie' – *"Sexy Sadie/ Look what you've done/ You've made a fool of everyone"* – and it quickly became common knowledge that the person concealed behind the phrase 'sexy Sadie' was the Maharishi.

With the Beatles back in England, work was immediately begun on the next album. However, many of the songs had been written in India – and hence in contemplative isolation. Although Lennon and McCartney had composed more or less separately for some time, there had usually been some form of collaboration at the recording stage. Thus, for example, it is clear that 'A Day In The Life' on *Sergeant Pepper* is a song to which each of them made decisive contributions. Now, however, such collaboration was at an end. Songs that had been written separately were also recorded separately. The old idea of the Beatles as a complete, self-sufficient group changed dramatically. Now they were working individually, as often as not in different studios at Abbey Road, recording their contributions separately, with George Martin simply overseeing the entire project. (Hence his role was far less central than it had ever been, and he was relegated from artistic interpreter to technical dogsbody. There was a definite reason for this, which had nothing to do with Martin himself. When *Sergeant Pepper* had been released, one reviewer had written, "This is George Martin's best album yet . . ." The Beatles never forgot that, and Martin was victimised because of it. When the White Album was finally issued, he received no producer's credit, just a curt thank-you, in a small type-size, en bloc with a host of other people whose contributions would have been far more peripheral.)

Jeff Lynne, leader of the Electric Light Orchestra, recalled a visit to the studios at the time the Beatles were in session there: "There's John Lennon and George Harrison sitting there, and George Martin's conducting this orchestra. They were doing this song called 'Glass Onion'. Then I went into this other studio where there was a session going on with Paul McCartney, and he was doing 'Why Don't We Do It In The Road?'. I wish he'd been doing something a bit better, but you can't have everything."

The centrifugal tendencies were already so strong that Harrison could not even persuade the others to turn up at the studios to record 'While My Guitar Gently Weeps' with him, and that is why it was recorded with Eric Clapton and others.

It was while they were recording *The Beatles* that a more fundamental change in the composition of the group circle took place. With long nights in the studio ahead of him, John had sent Cynthia back on holiday following their return from the Maharishi's centre at Rishikesh. Two weeks later, she arrived back from Greece to discover Yoko Ono installed in their house in St George's Hill, Weybridge. A few weeks later, on yet another holiday with Julian and her mother to escape the unpleasant atmosphere at home Cynthia was greeted by Alexis Mardas, who had been despatched to inform her that John wanted a divorce and custody of their son. (The former presented few problems; the latter, even John had to accept, was impossible.)

The John and Yoko relationship had been slow to develop, since they had first met in November 1966 at an art exhibition organised by John Dunbar, Marianne Faithfull's ex-husband. Yoko was not especially aware of the Beatles, and was unfamiliar with their music, but from then on a clandestine relationship began to develop. Yoko kept in touch with John, either by mailing him postcards or, on several occasions, turning up uninvited at his Weybridge home, although she never gained admittance. John was intrigued, however, and sponsored an exhibition of hers in September 1967.

The contact between them subsequently increased, so that by the time John went to the Maharishi's meditation centre, Yoko was regularly air-mailing him missives containing her cryptic messages. It was while Cynthia was in Greece that John and Yoko first spent the night together. In the early morning they recorded an album, and thereafter remained virtually inseparable for the next five years.

It was this immediate development of a double identity which made the relationship so different to the John–Cynthia one, which had been conducted along traditional lines. Yoko had particular thoughts about feminism, and about male chauvinism, which had never been current in Beatle circles before. Indeed, they had all settled comfortably and naturally into traditional middle-class existences; while the men went out to work, the wives stayed in, minding the home and the family.

In the beginning, John had enjoyed three close relationships: there was Cynthia, his girlfriend; Paul, in whom he had discovered the perfect working partner and with whom he was able to share all his musical interests; and Stu Sutcliffe, the talented student whom John had met when they were both registered at the Liverpool College of Art. John was never ambitious simply to be a musician, even if that was his over-riding ambition. He had always wanted to be a writer and an artist as well, and it was in Stu's company that he was able to slake his thirst for intellectual and aesthetic pursuits. Stu's knowledge of and absorption in Art fired him greatly. To quote Philip Norman: "Van Gogh, even more than Elvis Presley, now became the hero against whom John Lennon measured the world."

He lost Stu straightaway. After one of the Beatles' Hamburg engagements, Stu opted to remain behind with his fiancée, Astrid Kirchherr, and to study at the local art college under the renowned Edouardo Paolozzi. He died of cerebral paralysis on April 10 1962. John felt, but naturally did not show, a great sense of loss. Up to the end he had been hoping to persuade Stu to rejoin the Beatles as bass guitarist, even though it was neither a metier which suited Stu nor a satisfactory arrangement for the group.

It is, therefore, true to say that when John first became fascinated with Yoko, she not only abrogated to herself the different functions previously served by Cynthia and Paul. She was also perfectly equipped to take the long-vacant place of Stu in John's life.

Yoko, then, wanted to be a partner of John's in both his working and his home life. John, for his part, became instantly receptive to Yoko's ideas about Art. Art is all around, everything is Art. That was her feeling. Yoko imagined that creativity was boundless and immediate, and that it somehow arrived without labour pains. John was hooked; he'd never liked hard work anyway, and he ignored for the moment the difficulty of following through the proposition that if artistic instincts were really spread as democratically as Yoko maintained, then he could hardly be the supreme individual genius he thought he was.

For Yoko, of course, there was little point to her art unless it attracted wide publicity. If one was going to challenge received attitudes and traditional values in advanced industrial societies then one may as well do it with the aid of the full communications panoply of advanced industrial societies. Now, if Art could be something simple, like, say, a Happening, then it followed that the greater the publicity, the greater the happening, the greater the Art. John Lennon could generate such publicity effortlessly. Irrespective of whether or not he deliberately determined to create it, John Lennon was news.

The John and Yoko relationship had been a long time in gestation, but when it finally blasted off, it shot up with unerring speed, power and accuracy: rather like the Columbia space shuttle, in fact. Within weeks, the John–Yoko partnership was one of the most notorious in the Western world; but if their actions bemused and offended the general public, the other three Beatles were no less affronted.

Ever since the beginning, the four had formed a close-knit group, and most of those who penetrated the inner sanctum were all associates who survived from the years before nationwide fame. All of the Beatle wives/girlfriends responded to the male/female stereotypes that had been ingrained in them from birth. (Cynthia Lennon recalls that Ringo's wife Maureen would always ensure that he had a roast dinner waiting for him whenever he came home from work at the recording studio – whatever hour of the day or night that happened to be.) All remained in the background, never presuming either to assist their partner in his work or to assert their own independence. Indeed, it was this last factor that caused the break-up of the Paul McCartney–Jane Asher relationship.

Therefore, when John introduced Yoko into the cosy circle, he broke all the unwritten, but well-established, rules. In some obscure way they could not articulate, they felt that John had betrayed the sanctity of the union, and broken the Beatle bond. They were all shocked, and inevitably reacted to Yoko's intrusion with a cool detachment or a sullen hostility that took years to overcome. That Yoko should have been emboldened to put in an appearance at the studios while recording of *The Beatles* was in progress was something they could not easily forgive.

Cynthia, meanwhile, was abruptly left out in the cold. The others hardly knew how to react. George and Ringo hardly saw her again; not, at least, for several years. Paul did drive down to comfort her and Julian – an occasion famous in Beatle mythology since it

was on that journey that he composed a comforting song, 'Hey, Jules', the title of which he subsequently altered to 'Hey, Jude'. Later on, he paid another visit, with Linda, during which he took photographs of Julian to take back to John. Such social niceties were, however, the exception, and the virtual ostracism of Cynthia was symbolic not just of the break-up of John's marriage, but of the dissolution of the group. (Cynthia says that she considered the unsociable atmosphere absurd and, in an attempt to restore harmonious relations, hosted a party at the Kensington home where she had moved from Weybridge. It was to be one of the few times when she met Yoko, although the occasion, as she remembers it, was disastrous and never to be repeated.)

Against this background of incipient disharmony, the most ironic aspect of *The Beatles* was its title. They'd never used the name of the group to stand as the album-title before, and now that they had it was on the least appropriate occasion. The double-album was clearly the work of four separate artistes, not a cohesive unit. Though the usual device of crediting songs to the Lennon–McCartney team was retained, it was by now child's play to distinguish a Lennon composition from a McCartney one.

The album was, however, given the customary rapturous welcome. There were some quibbles that a double album seemed over-long, but these were rather unfair. After all, *The Beatles* did cover a vast canvas, and included affectionate pastiches of a range of popular music styles. There was even space for 'Revolution No. 9', a lengthy free-form exercise in tape-loops from Lennon that perfectly illustrated his determination not to

Though they offered little initial assistance to 'Yellow Submarine', when they realised how good it was, the Beatles opted for a full-length soundtrack.

recognise artistic boundaries (and which sounded to thousands of listeners a self-indulgent waste of vinyl).

The album was released in good time to take advantage of the Christmas market – which was just as well, because for the first time in their history the group had no Christmas single to offer. Nevertheless, Beatlemaniacs would still have been out-of-pocket, with four album relases from the group members in those few weeks at the end of 1968.

One of these was the soundtrack of the *Yellow Submarine* cartoon film. This was a project which had been sanctioned by Brian Epstein in 1966, but the Beatles themselves had been greatly disturbed by the enterprise, and would no doubt have aborted it had they been able. As it was, they offered virtually no ideas or assistance, and became accustomed to setting aside inferior material to go towards the soundtrack they were supposed to be doing. In the event, there were four new songs, one of which George Harrison was obliged to write and record on the spot because, despite their precautions, they were desperately short of material. Since the song concerned, 'Only A Northern Song' had considerable merit, one wonders why Harrison has not since been encouraged to compose at a less stately pace.

The Beatles had originally planned to release the songs as an EP, but once they'd seen the film, and realised how good it was, they felt that a full-length soundtrack would be more appropriate. Probably this was the wrong reaction, at least for a British audience: the film had preceded the album by six months, and fans who had been looking forward to purchasing the new songs felt cheated that they were only available as part of an album, one side of which didn't contain Beatle music at all (but the George Martin orchestral score for the film). Hence, the album sold disappointingly in the U.K., although amazingly well in the U.S.

The other two items of Beatle product had been George Harrison's *Wonderwall* soundtrack album – mostly sitar music to accompany a spirit of '67 psychedelic movie. The most accomplished pieces were those that George had recorded in Bombay with other Indian musicians. From John and Yoko there was *Two Virgins*, the cover of which featured them both in full frontal pose. Polite society was scandalised, as indeed it had been ever since the inception of the John and Yoko affair. Although Yoko was inevitably held to be the villain of the piece, there was a feeling too that Lennon had lost his marbles. As the two planted acorns at Coventry Cathedral, and organised art exhibitions on subjects that seemed to have little in common with conventional notions of Art (John arranged a show of charity collection boxes), so an antagonistic press fanned the flame of public

October, 1968. John and Yoko arrested on drugs charges in Ringo's Montagu Square apartment

hostility. In October, the two of them were arrested on drugs charges at the flat in Montagu Square which Ringo owned, and to which they had moved from Weybridge. This single, relatively innocuous incident was to have repercussions that no-one could have envisaged at the time.

It was certainly the sort of incident that would have been unthinkable during Brian Epstein's lifetime. He had always been fastidious in protecting his charges against just that sort of difficulty. Now that it had occurred, the public were hardly surprised; to them it simply confirmed all their least kind prejudices about the kind of transformation that had taken place in John since his liaison with Yoko. There was thus little sympathy when Yoko lost the baby they had been expecting – the more so since John, acting entirely contrary to the paternalistic attitudes that had prevailed within the group from the outset, had slept beside Yoko in Queen Charlotte hospital when she had her miscarriage.

The whole Beatles legend of invulnerability began to fall apart, and the ill-fated Apple enterprise only accelerated this process or erosion. Apple had begun, while Epstein was still alive, as a boutique in Baker Street, which had been a total disaster. Though it and had been a total disaster. Though it designs to which other local businessmen had objected – somewhat hypocritically, since all the publicity could only benefit the neighbourhood), the Beatles had decided that the rag trade wasn't for them – whatever made them think that it was? – and closed it down the following summer, giving away the shop's entire stock.

The Apple organisation itself – Apple Corps Ltd – had begun operating in April 1968. Its purpose was supposedly to promote undernourished talents of all kinds, everywhere.

Lennon and McCartney had undertaken a promotional trip to New York together to announce its inception. "It will be a sort of 'Western communism'," McCartney, that most conservative of rock stars, blithely announced.

Only the truly naïve could have failed to foresee what would happen. The Beatles were inundated. All manner of tapes and manuscripts flooded in to Apple, and the offices themselves became the mecca for assorted hangers-on and freelance scroungers of the Western world, who undermined and then destroyed the essential worthiness of the original plan.

Of course, the Beatles were complete novices in affairs of business, and since Brian Epstein's death some months earlier there wasn't even any managerial guidance forthcoming. Apple was an enterprise into which they ran blindly. Though not entirely a tax loss, it was begun at a time when accountants were telling them that they had to dispose of sums in excess of £2 million, else if it would all go to the Inland Revenue. Leaving this aside, however, one can say that the primary inspiration for Apple was the altruistic one of wanting to make readily available to others all the business advantages which they had procured so painstakingly. No doubt they still recalled the times when London seemed a million miles away, and their chances of ever obtaining a recording contract were equally remote. Further, of course, there was the desire of the Beatles – and particularly McCartney – not only to establish themselves as wide-ranging artistes capable of expressing themselves in any art form, but also to act as patrons and progenitors of a general cultural movement.

In casting themselves in the roles both of Leonardo on the one hand and the Medicis on the other, the Beatles were indubitably

By 1969 the dream is over

asking too much of themselves. Even so, one imagines that Apple may well have had more chance of success had it been graced with a less charlatan business atmosphere. In believing (quite rightly) that certain traditional business practices were not only demeaning in human terms but moribund anyway, the Beatles went too far and discarded all conventional precepts of running a company. It was one thing to believe that nine-to-five was an outdated concept, and another to allow the Apple offices to become a permanent party venue.

Having informed the world only the previous year that All You Need Is Love, the Beatles no doubt believed that they could make it happen like that. Although the whole Apple fiasco has subsequently become a source of great humour (which was perfectly exploited in, for example, *The Rutles*), in reality it affords one no satisfaction to admit that such a grand and idealistic enterprise could be brought to its knees so rapidly because certain Apple employees, betraying the faith and trust that had been placed in them, exploded the all-you-need-is-love attitude in the Beatles' face.

The only other thing to mention is that the ill-fated Apple business contrasted strikingly with the way the group handled their own immediate affairs. They may have been naïve and idealistic in the broad sense. When dealing with their own merchandise, however, the Beatles were unerringly shrewd and business-like. Albums were consistently released at an opportune moment in late autumn to achieve maximum commercial effect, for example. In general, they nearly always behaved with an awareness of the needs of the market-place and an astute understanding of how to maximise sales and profits.

Apple's publishing business was stillborn,

and its films division barely got off the ground. Only the recording company seemed destined to achieve its aims, since the Beatles had not only taken the precaution of signing themselves to the label, but had also brought in as one of their first artistes Mary Hopkin, the winner of a television talent competition, who, under Paul's guidance, notched up a respectable quota of Top 10 hits. These included her debut single, 'Those Were The Days', which Paul had produced for her and which replaced 'Hey, Jude' at No. 1 in the U.K. singles charts, and only reached No. 2 in the U.S. because 'Hey, Jude' held on at No. 1 for a record-breaking ten weeks.

Apple's A&R man was Peter Asher, who had for years looked destined to become Paul's brother-in-law. That eventuality never came to pass, and neither did his appointment at Apple ever blossom as it might have done, which was a shame because the Beatles had undoubtedly got the right man for the job. He quickly became disillusioned and moved to California with his protégé, James Taylor, to become manager/producer both for him and for Linda Ronstadt.

James Taylor is just one of the many names that Apple could have had on its books. It is pointless to speculate, of course, but since virtually every promising new artiste wanted to sign for the Beatles' label, it is no exaggeration to say that Apple could easily have become the major recording company of the '70s. As well as Taylor, they might have had Supertramp, Poco (who changed their name from Pogo on the advice of John Lennon) and Hot Chocolate, who were actually christened by one of the Apple secretaries.

It was not to be. Apple was mayhem. It was another of the major flaws in the Beatles' grand design that surely would have been avoided if Brian Epstein had survived.

CHAPTER 2

End Of A Dream

By 1969 the dream was almost over. Despite all they had achieved, they were still subject to their own heavy work schedule – or, rather, the one imposed on them by McCartney, for as usual it was he who chivvied the others into sustained activity.

The project that was initiated at Twickenham Studios in the early morning of January 2 1969 was conceptualised as a multi-media Beatle assignment. Cameras would record the group in the throes of recording a new album, which would then be released in conjunction with the film and a book.

Film, record, book; why make money in one field when you can do it in three? For all the 'Western communism' of Apple, for all the professed spiritual proclivities of George in particular and the others in general, for all that the Beatles had been the prime factor in inspiring an adolescent backlash against the conventions of materialist society – they continued to work the strings of commercialism.

The basic theme behind this particular project was indicated by the title of Paul's song 'Get Back'. The whole point of inviting the cameras into their recording sessions was that the group would be 'live' in the studio. The intention was to demonstrate that despite all the technological nuances that they and George Martin had developed and popularised, they could still be raw and earthy as occasion demanded.

Since they had stopped touring in 1966, the Beatles had been slightly piqued by accusations that they could function effectively only with the assistance of (a.) the accoutrements of the recording studio and (b.) George Martin. 'Get Back' would thus mark a return to their roots, and would enable them to rediscover not only the urgency they had possessed in their Cavern days, but also – Paul no doubt fondly hoped – the sense of comradeship that had been such a vital factor of those performances.

In the event, the 'Get Back' sessions failed to fulfil the first aim; and the caustic and disputatious atmosphere in which they were quickly immersed made a complete mockery of the second.

The whole Beatles legend began to fall apart and the ill-fated Apple enterprise accelerated the process. 'It will be a sort of Western communism,' Paul had stated. In fact the fiasco served to explode the 'all-you-need-is-love' attitude.

It became clear that the concept of 'the Beatles' meant something different to each of them. To Paul, it meant the opportunity to pursue ever greater artistic triumphs; to Ringo, it just meant a kind of happy, successful family; to George, it represented the method whereby his creativity and opportunities for artistic development were shackled, and to John it just represented some kind of superannuated pop group.

Against such a background, the sessions were a disaster. They were conducted in difficult circumstances, anyway. The Beatles found it hard to be inspired working in front of the cameras, and those huge lights, and at such unaccustomed times of the day.

Paul and George frequently argued, and John could no longer even feign interest in the proceedings. Ringo, who had for so long been the calm of the centre of the storm, the one constant factor keeping those mercurial artistic sensibilities in some sort of harmony, was now unable to arrest the forces of disintegration.

In any case the concept itself was mistaken. It was as difficult for the Beatles themselves to recognise intimations of artistic mortality as it was for their most devoted fans. They'd always prided themselves – quite justifiably – on their recording perfection. Hence, what they now tried to achieve was a deliberately live sound, but one which didn't conflict with their usual standards of perfectionism. The elements of the prescription were impossibly contradictory, and it is small wonder that the sessions became increasingly fraught and rancorous.

They were duly concluded, with no-one knowing what to do with the taped material that had been amassed. None of them were in any way satisfied with it, though Lennon, at least, seemed to feel that it would be instructive to release the tapes exactly as they were, so that people could hear the Beatles *au natural*, without benefit of studio cosmetics, "with our trousers down," said Lennon. (It is thus another of the amazing contradictions of the Beatles' story that it was he who finally arranged for the tapes to be doctored far more artificially than any other Beatles' recording.)

To begin with, though, the theme did hold up, and 'Get Back' was coupled with John's 'Don't Let Me Down' for the next group single, which was released in April 1969 and promoted under the line, "The Beatles . . . as nature intended." In order fully to demonstrate that there had been no sleight-of-hand Billy Preston was personally credited for his keyboard contributions, thus becoming one of the very few outside musicians ever to be so honoured by the group.

The song had been performed live on the roof of the Apple offices in Savile Row, and was to represent the last ever semi-public appearance of the Beatles as a group. The occasion itself, however, was the product more of prevarication than of purposefulness. All through 1968 there had been hints that the band would do more live appearances, but in the end they were so much at odds that this became yet another topic on which unanimous agreement was impossible. So the rooftop concert was the shabby compromise, so characteristic of this tetchy period of Beatle history. It is equally necessary to affirm, however, that, as in everything (*everything*) connected with the Beatles, this too had a magic of its own, and will be remembered positively, as another of the Fab Four's loony but loveable stunts.

Such displays of unity, faltering as they were, contrasted starkly with what was actually happening, namely that the stage was being cleared for the final denouement. As the bonds of Beatle brotherhood were

irreparably broken, two distinct camps emerged, with John, Yoko and Allen Klein ranged on one side, and Paul and the Eastman family on the other.

Paul had originally become acquainted with Linda Eastman, a New York photographer, when she had inveigled her way into a *Sergeant Pepper* promotional photo-session. Their friendship had been renewed when Paul and John had flown over to launch Apple in the Big Apple. After Paul's separation from Jane Asher, the relationship was able to ripen; Linda and her six-year-old daughter, Heather, moved in with Paul in November 1968, and they got married on March 12 the following year. In the same way that John had found an ideal partner in Yoko, who was able to combine within herself the separate functions previously served by Cynthia and Paul, so Paul himself had found what he felt he needed all along: a home-lovin' woman, who was prepared to devote herself exclusively to her husband's family and his career.

There had always been order and discipline in Paul's home life. Obviously, all four Beatles had strong family roots back home in Liverpool, and that was one vital factor which facilitated their survival, relatively unscathed, of the years of Beatlemania. Equally obviously, however, the four knew different degrees of affinity with their home background, and Paul's family ties were always the strongest. He appreciated this himself, and could rapturise endlessly about the blessings of family life; 'Let 'Em In', one of the tracks from *Wings At The Speed Of Sound*, perfectly captures this attitude; he addresses many members of his family by name, and extends an open invitation to them all.

"It probably is schmaltzy," he told the *Sunday Times* (April 1976). "I'm from that

17th February, 1969. Linda Eastman first photographed with Paul.

sort of family. We were very close, with aunties and uncles always coming in, sing-songs and parties. I saw John and Yoko last time I was in New York and I happened to mention for some reason our family sing-songs. He said he never had them. He didn't have the sort of family life I had. Yoko didn't either, she had to make appointments to see her dad. I now realise how lucky I am to have a close, loving family."

It is hardly surprising that a close, loving family is what he wanted for himself, and in

12th March, 1969. The last bachelor
Beatle marries and avoids the weeping
fans by entering Marylebone Registry
Office by a side entrance.

the end it was a difference of opinion over
when to start building one that caused the
rupture of his long relationship with Jane
Asher. The disagreement was merely the
surface indication of a great divide, for Jane
possessed a fierce independence of mind and
spirit that hardly dovetailed with Paul's
conception of an ordered family life. "Jane
had her own highly successful stage and film
career. With her angelic looks went a strong
mind and forthright manner, which curtailed
Paul's ego and deflated his superstar pom-

posities." (Philip Norman – *Shout! The True
Story Of The Beatles*).

No sooner had Jane exited stage left, than
Linda made her entrance from the opposite
side.

Linda suited Paul perfectly. Not only was
she prepared to embark on family life from
the outset, she had already done so, since she
had a six-year-old daughter, Heather (who
had been born on December 31 1963), and
the two were soon installed at Paul's St.
John's Wood home.

She was the perfect partner in other ways, she had some kudos in her own right, coming from a well-to-do U.S. family on the Eastern seaboard which had a 5th Avenue business address, while she was also prepared to be utterly devoted to Paul, and would be as domesticated as he wished her to be. "Most of all," writes Norman, "she idolised and pampered him in precisely the way Jane had always refused to do."

In retrospect, the fact that Paul should have composed the soundtrack music to *The Family Way* is absolutely appropriate. The family life of Paul and Linda has become noted for its cosy security and its standards of frugality, utterly flabbergasting for one of the country's wealthiest couples. No sooner had Linda presented Paul with a sizeable family of his own – with Mary (born August 28 1969), Stella (September 13 1971) and James (September 12 1977) – than all six moved to smaller accommodation, a two-bedroomed house near Rye in Sussex.

The arrival of the McCartneys in the area was hardly the boost to local employment prospects that some may initially have anticipated. They took on menial help sparingly, and if possible not at all. Linda prepared the meals herself (chores for which she was repaid with a song dedicated to her – 'Cook Of The House'), and undertook most of the housework. She bought the children's clothes at Mothercare, and drove them to school in her Mini. All in all, Paul went to extraordinary lengths to ensure that his wealth would not interfere with what he perceived to be the simple pleasures of family life.

Thus both John and Paul coincidentally became more emotionally independent of the other at almost the same time. Suddenly, they were no longer mutually reliant on the other's guidance, inspiration and competitive spirit.

This situation alone need not have generated implacable hostility between them, even though Paul (as well as George and Ringo) had resented Yoko's presence during recording sessions. It was, however, compounded by a basic business disagreement.

In January 1969 John Lennon had publicly stated that Apple was in bad financial shape – fast hurtling towards fiscal fade-out, in fact – as a direct result of which Allen Klein had presented himself at 3, Savile Row, Apple's London offices in Mayfair. Klein was a chunky New Yorker who had been associated frequently notoriously, with the record business for over a decade through his company ABKCO Productions. Though manager of the Rolling Stones, he'd never been satisfied with second-best, and had always cherished hopes of landing the biggest fish of them all.

It wasn't merely Klein's reputation that caused Paul to demur when the others presented his case. Equally important was the fact that he had been entertaining hopes of putting the Beatles' financial affairs into the hands of the Eastman family firm: Linda's father, Lee, and brother John.

Initially, the Beatles were open-minded about the situation, and a meeting was arranged at Apple with both Klein and the Eastmans, at which three factors tilted the balance in the former's favour. First of all Lee Eastman himself didn't attend, but sent his son John instead. The Beatles, accustomed as they were to being treated like royalty, felt slighted by Eastman Snr.'s aloofness.

His absence proved to be a gaffe in another respect, because John proved a raw envoy and lost his cool completely when confronted by Klein who, for once in his life, played the part of a kitten. The third factor, and Klein's ace, was that he only asked to take 20% only *future* earnings – i.e. of all the monies that he personally guaranteed to make for the

20th March, 1969, John marries Yoko. Coincidentally, John and Paul had become emotionally independent of each other at about the same time.

group, and he pledged not to touch the millions they had already made for themselves (and which, of course, were still arriving at Apple H.Q.).

Thus John was persuaded, and George and Ringo were of like mind. Klein was invited to take over their affairs. Apple, that putative bastion of Western communism, had found its Stalin.

Paul resisted signing managerial documents, although in fact Klein set to work as though he was managing the four of them, and McCartney was certainly able to take advantage of the vastly-improved royalty terms which Klein subsequently negotiated on his behalf.

Klein made a great display of this early victory against the forces of avaricious capitalism. That was nonsense. The 'victory' was there for the taking anyway. No-one disputed the rightness of the Beatles claim, least of all EMI, who knew that the group who had single-handedly transformed their worldwide trading position had been under-rewarded throughout. As the Chairman of Capitol (EMI's U.S. subsidiary) commented after the negotiations had been completed, "We'd have paid up anyway, so why did Klein have to be so nasty about it?"

In any case, the other major battles of the period were lost. Control of NEMS (Brian Epstein's management company) passed to Triumph Investment Trust; but even more alarmingly, Sir Lew Grade (now Lord Grade) of ATV gained control of the original Lennon-McCartney songwriting company, Northern Songs, and all the best endeavours of Klein and the four Beatles could not wrest it from him.

It is perhaps hard to credit the particular animosity of the Beatles towards Lew Grade. After all, Northern Songs had gone public in 1965, with the result (a) that Lennon and McCartney became millionaires overnight and (b) that shares were now freely available to anyone prepared to pay the asking price for them. Thus, they could hardly have been taken by complete surprise when Northern Songs did become the object of a takeover battle. John was utterly dismayed: "I'm not going to be fucked around by men in suits sitting on their fat arses in the city," he said. But it was the fact that it had to be Grade that really grated. After all, he was the epitome of the fat, cigar-smoking businessmen, the very breed that John in particular, as he entered his period of social and political concern, wanted to put out of existence altogether. Secondly, he represented the entertainment industry of yore – entertainment as good, clean schmaltz, with positively no distracting didacticism – which once again was something that the Beatles had wanted to supercede through the sheer excellence of their music. That the Beatles' music should be ensnared by such a man caused near apoplexy in the four of them, and they fought bitterly to prevent the successful conclusion of his takeover bid. Later on, of course, the Beatles overcame what, in a different atmosphere, began to seem like mere prejudices, and both Paul and John undertook engagements in connection with Grade in the '70s.

As for Apple itself – well, no-one could deny that Klein brought to his new job a sharp business sense. Suddenly it was clean-up time at Apple, as deceitful hangers-on and innocuous parasites alike found themselves out in the cold. A similar fate befell even many of those on the official Apple payroll (people like Alistair Taylor, Epstein's faithful retainer), who were brusquely informed that their services were no longer required.

Apple suddenly seemed like an abattoir and the Beatles themselves, not keen to bite this or any other bullet, stayed away.

One way and another, McCartney felt justified in leaving his financial affairs in the hands of the Eastmans – and that, since most of the business obviously concerned the four of them together, led to bizarre and tedious complications.

Both of the takeover battles had originated because individuals long associated with the group (in the case of NEMS, it was Brian's brother, Clive Epstein, and in the case of Northern Songs it was Dick James) had become unable to place their trust in its affairs any longer. Their unease had been induced partly by the appointment of Allen

Klein – whom many people after all regarded with quite justified suspicion – and partly by John Lennon's erratic behaviour.

Even by Beatle standards, the year had been a dramatic one for Lennon. Nicholas Schaffner in *The Beatles Forever* has pointed out that whereas McCartney got married in the full glare of publicity, but then honeymooned in private, Lennon did it the opposite way round. John's wedding in Gibraltar was a very private affair (Peter Brown flew out to be best man, and an English photographer, David Nutter, was summoned); but the honeymoon was shared with millions, as

JOHN LENNON

Before the Beatles bubble had burst, John received an invitation to attend a Toronto rock 'n' roll revival festival. It became the first live performance of the Plastic Ono Band, which then comprised John (guitar and vocals), Yoko (warblings), Eric Clapton (guitar), Alan White (drums) and Klaus Voormann (bass). The excitement of this triumphant gig was captured on *Plastic Ono Band – Live Peace in Toronto*.

Imagine, his first real solo album, was released in 1971. Probably his best, it was frighteningly intense, and for the next four years he remained in a virtually continuous state of conflict within himself (as he strove to extirpate his Beatle role and succeed as an individual), with the authorities (who saw him as a dangerous tool of the radical left), and at one stage with Yoko. When, in 1975, he regained his equilibrium, he announced: 'I'm not going to work for five years; I'm going to look after the baby.' In fact he returned from this self-imposed exile in time to record *Double Fantasy* for Sean's fifth birthday.

Gimme some truth . . .

John and Yoko spent it in bed in suite 902 of the Amsterdam Hilton, and invited along the world's press.

Once the media representatives had recovered from their initial disappointment (John and Yoko may have been in bed, but coitus was, alas, interruptus, so the story wasn't *that* good), they faithfully reported the couple's earnest protestations that they were doing all this in the cause of promoting world peace. Undeniably the publicity they generated for the cause was astonishing – as a publicist, Yoko had few peers – but the attention was not all good-natured, and suggestions that Lennon had become unhinged became commonplace.

The Amsterdam bed-in was followed by a trip to Vienna, for the screening on Austrian television of one of their films, *Rape*. (John and Yoko had assumed an immediate dominance over all art-forms. Records, films, sculpture; you name it, they could supply it. Tomorrow.) The occasion provided the best opportunity to date of a practical demonstration of 'bagism'. Most of us were perplexed about the precise merits of this particular form of activity, but apparently the idea had germinated from the theme of Antoine de Saint-Exupery's *The Little Prince*, 'the essential is invisible to the eye'. Anyway, John and Yoko, eating chocolate gateau with an impunity known only to the invisible, publicised their film from inside a bag at the Sacher hotel.

Other newsworthy activities ensued at weekly intervals: John changed his middle

Soon after they married, John and Yoko take to their bed in the Presidential suite of the Amsterdam Hilton for a 7-day protest against war and violence. It took a Portuguese chamber maid to interrupt the affair.

name from 'Winston' to 'Ono' in a ceremony on the roof of the Apple building; the pair of them released their second joint album, *Life With The Lions*, the front cover of which displayed a photograph of the two of them in Queen Charlotte hospital, and the back cover a news picture of them arriving at court on the drugs charge. They then made an unsuccessful attempt to join the QE2 on a transatlantic crossing, since Ringo and Peter Sellers were on board filming *The Magic Christian*.

They were also thwarted in attempts to enter the United States because of the drugs conviction, so they went to Canada instead for the second stage of their peace protest, holding a seven-day bed-in at a Montreal hotel. The city was selected for its proximity to the U.S. border, and the result was that this event generated even more world-wide publicity than the first one. John and Yoko's suite was permanently filled with media representatives and assorted celebrities.

There are two points of interest to mention. First of all, John would emerge from such week-long stints in bed physically exhausted, just because of the incessant activity and pressure. Secondly, although he was often castigated for what was felt to be naïve politicising, he himself remained acutely aware both of the inherent humour in the situation (that two people spending their time in bed should be so newsworthy was, after all, illogical and absurd), and also of the practical limitations of what they were doing. He nevertheless believed that for simple messages of peace to replace the cold-hearted duplicity of politicians in the headlines, if only for a few days, represented some kind of victory over the forces of darkness.

The Montreal bed-in, however, did produce a contribution of some permanence to the peace movement, and that was the song – or, perhaps, the refrain – 'Give Peace A Chance'. This was written on site, and recorded straightaway with everyone who happened to be in the room at the time: Tommy Smothers, Timothy Leary, the Canadian Radna Krishna Temple, *et al.* The song was issued at the beginning of July 1969, the first-ever single released by one of the Beatles independently. It was credited to the Plastic Ono Band, a non-existent group to which John gave some material form by putting together a quartet of transparent perspex robots, who subsequently made a live appearance at Chelsea Town Hall. Later on, of course, John used the term 'Plastic Ono Band' to refer to whoever was backing him on any particular project.

Just a few weeks prior to the release of 'Give Peace A Chance', John had provided another Beatles 45, 'The Ballad Of John And Yoko', which was to be the group's most uncharacteristic single. It catalogued noteworthy events in John and Yoko's crowded life from March to May, and was recorded solely by John and Paul; George was out of contact, and Ringo was away filming. As such, it represented one of the last attempts to keep the Beatles functioning as a group despite the increasing independence of the four.

'The Ballad Of John And Yoko' reached No. 1, of course, hitting the top soon after 'Get Back'. George was once again granted a concessionary B-side, 'Old Brown Shoe' (no sitars, and rather a good song). With all the activity on the recording front, fans may have been lulled into believing that the old dreadnought was serviceable yet.

Nevertheless, the solo activities were swelling daily. While Ringo was working on *The Magic Christian*, Paul was writing its title-song, the excellent 'Come And Get It', which he gave to one of Apple's first signings, the Iveys, whom he re-christened Badfinger.

RINGO STARR

Ringo had been the one constant factor in a turbulent sea of artistic sensibilities as the Beatles era neared its close. He was even the go-between when Paul's *McCartney* release threatened to clash head-on with the last offering from the Beatles. The break-up was clearly a major upset for him – Ringo's solo career seemed to have started by default. And if the burden of proving himself fell most heavily upon him, the reaction to his first two offerings – *Sentimental Journey* and *Beaucoups Of Blues* – must have disillusioned him further.

Three years after his second solo album he returned with a major success, appropriately entitled *Ringo* because it was so quintessentially him. In calling upon the assistance of John, Paul and George, he provided the ideal antidote to bitter feelings between John and Paul that were being publicly aired. But besides it being a humanising influence, the album demonstrated Ringo's particular genius – his eternal good nature and equanimity.

He began on his own with less reason for confidence than the others, has since suffered the tragedy of the death of close friends Marc Bolan, Keith Moon, and John. Like all the ex-Beatles, his record has been uneven, but during the transition and since he has remained unerringly himself, clearly enjoying everything that life has to offer. Of the four, it is Ringo's personality that has assured him continuing popularity into the '80s.

His film career had begun rather unsatis-
factorily too, with *Candy* in 1968, and though
a more substantial role with Peter Sellers in
The Magic Christian promised more, he
never really got to grips with the character –
the film was good in parts, but not a major
success. Following this, came the Western,
Blindman, but it was not until his role in
That'll Be The Day that he achieved any real
success. It was a triumph of natural acting (or
acting naturally), and though his next
venture, *Born To Boogie*, a documentary
film about Marc Bolan which Ringo directed
did not receive anything like the same
acclaim, at least it showed that he was more
in touch than his former colleagues with the
shift in the pop music scene since the Beatles
parted.

All four Beatles had their flops on going
solo, and, in actual fact Ringo's first success
came quite early. The 1971 single, 'It Don't
Come Easy' was interesting for a number of
reasons. First of all, the title betrayed his own
uncertainty about his personal future. He
had written it with contributions from the
other three Beatles in mind, but only George
was at this stage prepared to support him. As
it turned out, Ringo was certainly underestimating himself. 'It Don't Come Easy'
dispelled all intimations of inadequacy and
outsold singles from the other three issued
during the same period.

Acting naturally . . .

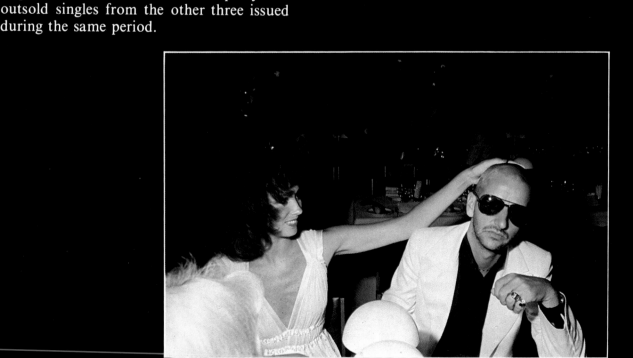

"I want a divorce – just like I had from Cynthia," said John

Of the four of them, only Paul and George seemed interested in treating Apple as a fully-functioning record company, rather than as an outlet for the Beatles' own product. Under Paul's aegis were Badfinger and Mary Hopkin, each of whom enjoyed intermittent success. George helped to boost the total number of Apple hits (right until the mid-'70s it had the highest percentage success rate of any U.K. record company) by producing 'That's The Way God Planned It' for Billy Preston and 'Hare Krishna' and 'Govinda' for the U.K. Radna Krishna Temple. He also worked less profitably on material by Jackie Lomax, Doris Troy and Ronnie Spector. There was also a second solo excursion of his own, *Electronic Sound* which, like the Lennons' *Life With The Lions*, appeared on the experimental, short-lived Zapple label.

The last-ever display of Beatle unity occurred during July and August 1969 when the four of them assembled at EMI's St John's Wood studios, where 16-track equipment was freshly installed, to record *Abbey Road*. Paul had set the wheels in motion by contacting George Martin. The latter had been reluctant to agree until everyone had promised to give their full co-operation and certainly to avoid the animosities that had clouded the atmosphere of the 'Get Back' sessions (the tapes of which were still unreleased).

In the event, the recording was completed quickly, smoothly and amicably, with quite beneficial results for one and all. Most people would point to *Abbey Road* as the ultimate affirmation of the collective genius of the Beatles. Despite all the bitterness of the 'Get Back' fiasco, the rows over Apple, the fact that they had all been working virtually separately throughout the year and that no material for the album had been rehearsed, it was a triumph.

Certainly, George had reason to feel satisfied, since his two allotted tracks, 'Something' and 'Here Comes The Sun', finally established him as a front-rank composer. 'Something' quickly settled in alongside 'Yesterday' and 'Can't Buy Me Love' as one of the classics of the Beatles canon, and in October became George's first-ever A-side single. He was dead chuffed. Recognition at last.

Side One featured a couple of jokey tracks – Ringo's re-write of 'Yellow Submarine' called 'Octopus's Garden', and Paul's 'Maxwell's Silver Hammer', which John, especially, loathed. Supposedly a song for the grannies, its psychopathic flavour made it ill-suited to its purpose.

There was only one other McCartney composition on Side One, 'Oh! Darlin'', but he had worked diligently and hard in putting together the suite of songs which comprises the lion's share of side two. This is a kind of pop symphony, with themes that recur throughout and are brought together at the end, interspersed with self-contained, abbreviated songs, only one of which, 'Polythene Pam', is Lennon's. It had long been an ambition of George Martin's to create just such a work, and to do it now seemed a fitting way of disposing of all the half-written songs that were otherwise destined to lie unheard in studio locker-rooms.

Because the Beatles were obviously reaching the end of the line.

John's contributions to *Abbey Road* were significantly few. His heart wasn't in it any more.

There were several reasons why his disillusionment had been brought to a head at this stage. He was disappointed that his two albums with Yoko had not received the full weight of an Apple promotional push. People in the company seemed to pay scant attention to them, and although one can imagine that they would find nothing appealing in them, John was hurt.

In retrospect, also, the birth of the Plastic Ono Band concept had hastened the demise of the Beatles. Although the P.O.B. had supposedly come into being simply as a channel into which John could divert all his compositions that didn't square with the Beatle image, the point is that those were the only kind of compositions he was now writing. For example, there was 'Cold Turkey', which he wrote after the conclusion of the *Abbey Road* sessions. It was a song he was excited about (and which he had hoped to record with Bob Dylan, after the latter had flown to John and Yoko's new home, Tittenhurst Park, at the end of the Isle of Wight festival; Dylan, however, wasn't interested), but it did seem neither melodic enough to be a Beatle single, nor appropriate lyrically.

Yoko had implanted in John a sense of her own spiritual and artistic self-sufficiency, and he found the feeling invigorating. During all the years of Beatle aggrandisement, Brian Epstein had kept a tight leash on Lennon, restraining him from the kind of wayward activities that had littered his chequered adolescence. Now, Lennon, suddenly finding himself unfettered, was behaving with unrestrained zest. In fact, all that now prevented him from becoming the kind of personality he'd always thought he wanted to be were the inhibitions imposed by his continued membership of the Beatles.

One day in the early autumn, when the four had met once again to discuss the continuing myriad problems that confronted them (the 'Get Back' tapes, Apple, Allen Klein, the whole future of the group), Lennon suddenly announced that he wanted out. "I want a divorce – just like I had from Cynthia." For the sake of the new contracts that Klein was

then still hammering out, for the sake of the various outstanding commitments hanging over them, Lennon was persuaded to say nothing publicly – although, effectively, his request was granted. The divorce from Cynthia had taken about six months to arrange, and the one from the Beatles took almost exactly the same time to come through.

It seemed, therefore, as though John had got what he wanted. Yet, in another sense, it was precisely what he didn't want. Despite the cushion of self-confidence which Yoko had provided for him, John still had his moments of understandable uncertainty and indecisiveness. To be a solo artiste was for him a new experience, and he'd take some time to come to terms with it. Previously, he'd always been the leader of a group, and had been emboldened in the collective security it provided. On his own, he'd feel unnerved, isolated, panic-struck, even.

Just before he'd communicated his decision to leave the Beatles, John had returned to live performance. Having received a last-minute invitation to attend the Toronto rock 'n' roll revival festival, he impulsively agreed to show up – but only if he could play a set (a condition which no doubt exceeded the wildest dreams of the organisers). John and Yoko duly arrived, together with the first incarnation proper of the Plastic Ono Band: Eric Clapton (guitar), Alan White (drums) and Klaus Voormann (bass). No group had ever been assembled more quickly, and since Lennon, who was sick with nerves in anticipation of the gig, had missed the flight he was supposed to catch, there was no time for orthodox rehearsals. Nevertheless, the spirit of rock 'n' roll triumphed, everybody had a good time, and the live album that was later released managed to capture the excitement of the occasion.

"'How I Won The War' was the first thing he'd done on his own - he was petrified,'' recalls Cynthia.

John was thrilled by the fact that he'd pulled it off, and had overcome his qualms about appearing on stage again. He was particularly struck by the fact that he'd managed to do it without the other Beatles, on whose support he had depended for his entire professional life.

This made is easier for him to announce to Paul, George and Ringo that he was leaving the group, because it meant that he had a ready-made alternative. This was the mental crutch he needed at the time, but it was not a solid support. Even though his fantasy Plastic Ono Band had now been given concrete form, it was still no more than an *ad hoc* band, and so what Lennon was really doing was committing himself to a solo career. This was a path that was far more fraught with difficulty for him than the public could have supposed at the time.

He'd never been good at doing things on his own. In the company of the Beatles his rapier wit had been equal to any occasion. But when, as an individual, he'd been expected to make a speech at a Foyle's literary luncheon he couldn't do it. He couldn't even be funny. Cynthia Lennon says that he was never a natural solo artiste. "When he was doing *How I Won The War*, he was petrified. It was the first thing he'd done on his own, and i was like leaving the family nest. He went through hell.

"He was the leader of a group, and in leaving the group he lost an awful lot of his strength."

His growing realisation that he was a Beatle apart is one reason that the songs on his debut album, *John Lennon/Plastic Ono Band*, were so harrowing; it is also significan that one of the tracks was entitled 'Isolation'

George too felt equally ill-at-ease in un familiar surrounding once he had ventured away from the Beatle abode for the first time He guested as guitarist on the December Delaney and Bonnie U.K. tour, although he declined to allow the fact to be publicised in any way. On stage, he stood behind the front line, and looked withdrawn and tentative. All the important guitar breaks were taken by Delaney and another guest, Eric Clapton. By then, of course, Harrison must have been wondering what he was going to do for the rest of his life.

The response of the others to 'Cold Turkey' had reinforced John's decision to quit, since they had shown no enthusiasm when he had proposed it as the next Beatles single release With Paul now running the show, John was becoming increasingly alienated, and his reaction was to issue the song under his own Plastic Ono Band banner, having recorded i with Clapton, Voormann and Ringo.

In the event, the commercial instinct of the others proved well-founded, because 'Cold Turkey' met an appropriately frosty recep tion from the record-buying public, and did poorly by Beatle standards. Later in the yea when John returned his MBE to Buckingham

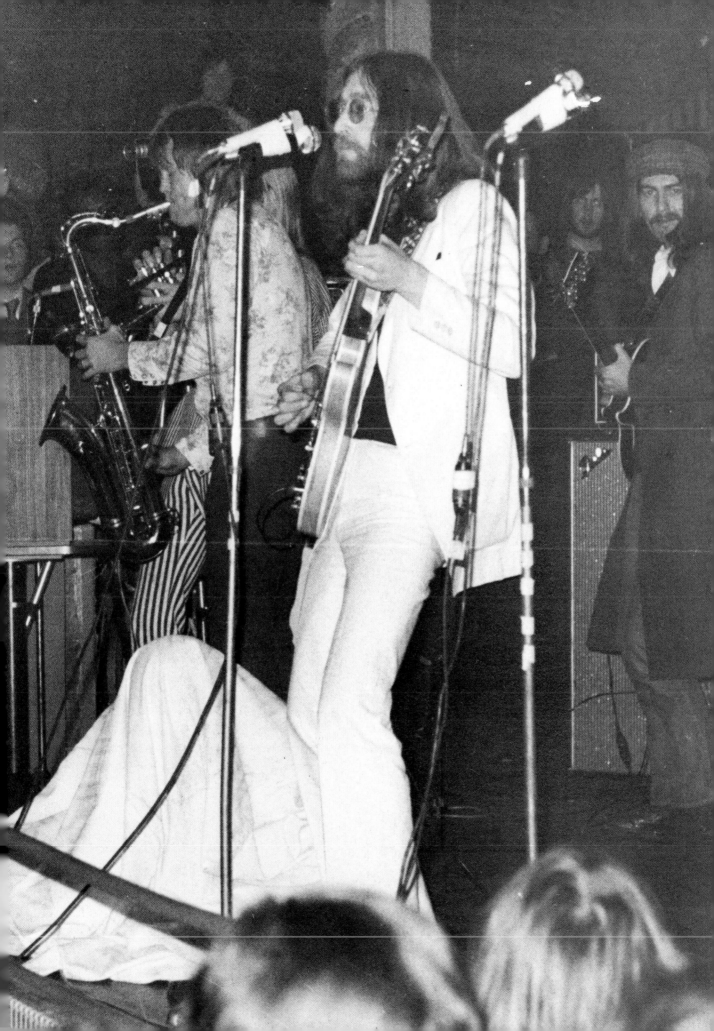

Palace, he gave as one of the reasons for doing so the fact that the single had been slipping down the charts. The jokey mention of 'Cold Turkey' – included, said Lennon, to stop the whole thing becoming too serious – was a happy reminder that however much he became involved with politics, he could never become boring.

The main reasons he gave for returning the honour were the continued support of the Harold Wilson government for America in Vietnam and for Nigeria in Biafra. Over and above that, the reason was probably just that it was time for another stunt.

His flippant reference to 'Cold Turkey' had deprived the action of the chance of achieving any political capital, though this possibility was infinitesimal anyway. Lennon admitted that he'd been looking for an opportunity to return the medal, but that doesn't mean to say that he'd found one when he did so. Had the action been tied precisely to some particular event, it might at least have focused public debate. Since it wasn't, it was a muddled and pointless gesture which naturally drew even more outrage than the original decoration in 1965 (when a number of stuffed shirts had returned *theirs* in protest).

The last weeks of the year were hectic even by the standards of Lennon's recent past. He brought his peace campaign to a climax, at considerable personal expense, by promoting his new slogan – WAR IS OVER (IF YOU WANT IT), signed Happy Xmas from John and Yoko – in full-page advertisements in the world's leading newspapers, and also on billboards in several capital cities.

On December 15, he and Yoko played a UNICEF benefit at the Lyceum ballroom in London, appearing with a Plastic Ono Supergroup, which boasted an array of famous names, including Keith Moon, Billy Preston, George Harrison and most of the Delaney and Bonnie entourage who were just then completing their own tour.

The next day, John and Yoko flew to Canada, ostensibly to make preparations for a massive music and peace festival that would be held near Toronto the following year. Once again, it proved perfect for their requirements since it generated enormous press coverage throughout North America. They stayed at Ronnie Hawkins' farm just outside Toronto. While there, and under the attention of a horde of pressmen, John spent much time signing a limited edition of erotic lithographs, which, Yoko assured him, established him as a leading artist ("better than Picasso"). He also appeared on television talking with the late Marshall McLuhan, and entertained Dick Gregory. The highlight of the visit, though, was a 50-minute audience with Canadian prime minister Pierre Trudeau, the very first time that Lennon had been received by an established politician in his capacity as peace campaigner, rather than as a Beatle.

The peace festival never happened, largely because, in the wake of the Rolling Stones' brutal Altamont performance, festivals never again seemed quite such a good idea; and nothing would undermine the credibility of a music and peace festival like knifings in front of the stage.

Nevertheless, it was the meeting with Trudeau that was of most importance. That remained a considerable coup for Lennon, and it was reinforced when he returned to England by the fact that BBC's *24 Hours* broadcast a documentary on him, and an ATV programme profiled him as one of three Men Of The Decade (the others were Chairman Mao and John F. Kennedy).

Perhaps, after all, he could survive without Paul, George and Ringo.

CHAPTER
3

Giving Peace A Chance

In January 1970 Phil Spector arrived in London in reasonable hope of fulfilling his greatest dream: producing the Beatles.

Spector, the greatest single name in record production, whose reputation overshadowed even that of George Martin, had been virtually a recluse for the second half of the '60s. Klein had now invited him back into the limelight because it was becoming increasingly apparent that the vexed question of the 'Get Back' tapes would have to be resolved, simply because so much money was tied up in the enterprise.

The Beatles themselves seemed disinclined to embark on any course of positive action. It was now over three months since John and Paul had spoken to each other, and none of the four visited the Apple offices with regularity. Klein, however, did know that John and George, particularly, both held Spector in especially high esteem.

When he arrived, Spector was quickly put to work. Not, though, on the long-delayed tapes, but on a new Lennon single, 'Instant Karma'. The song had been written in the

Paul fought hardest to keep the group intact – but finally he capitulated to the inevitable

morning of January 27, and John wished to record it in the afternoon, using Harrison, Klaus Voormann and Alan White as backing musicians, with Spector as co-producer. 'Instant Karma' was thus duly completed, and released ten days later. It was excellent. Lennon was characteristically simple and direct, but this time on a song with one of those magically catchy refrains.

Spector's production acumen was also evident; vocals, drums and keyboards all sounded especially effective. Nonetheless, Lennon's determination to compress the entire creative process into one working day was an essential factor, since it restrained Spector from further embellishing the record, in his characteristic style. This was something which he was keen to do, and which would almost certainly have detracted from its quality. As it was, the record reached the Top 5 in the U.K. and went gold in the U.S., thereby representing one of the most lucrative day's work that even John Lennon had undertaken.

There were never really any doubts about Spector's suitability for the job, but if there had been 'Instant Karma' would have dispelled them. Accordingly, the 'Get Back' tapes were handed over, and Spector was officially allotted the task of making them fit for public consumption. He was able to work unhindered; none of the Beatles interfered in any way, either directly or indirectly. The album, with its accompanying book, was scheduled for release in April, with the film following a month later.

Now, when Lennon had recorded 'Instant Karma' it hadn't really occurred to him that the Beatles were still in existence. To him, the group was already as dead as Monty Python's parrot. But there had never been a seal of dissolution, as it were, and the public still remained in blissful ignorance. The

denouement was provoked by Phil Spector. When Paul heard what had been done to 'The Long And Winding Road', he finally capitulated to the inevitable.

'The Long And Winding Road' had originally been written as an unpretentious ballad, a McCartney special, with just vocals and piano. In that manner, it was effectively performed in the *Let It Be* film. However, on sifting through the 'Get Back' material, Spector had clearly appreciated that 'The Long And Winding Road' offered him the only real opportunity of doing a big production job. So, the song was larded over with strings and choirs, and rendered virtually unlistenable.

It was not only McCartney who was shocked. The fans were also appalled. As a group, the Beatles had possessed innumerable virtues, not the least salient of which was the fact that they and Martin had consistently, and deliberately, eschewed the use of conventional, not to say hoary, production techniques.

Both McCartney and Martin felt crushed, and the former has always maintained that he did all he could to prevent the song's release in that form.

However, it was too late, and when the approach failed, he simply left the group. Both George and Ringo had each stalked out over the course of the previous years, though each had been coaxed back without difficulty; John had left the previous autumn, but had maintained an uncharacteristic silence in not publicising it. Now it was Paul's turn and ironically – since it was he who had always fought hardest to keep the group intact – it was he who told the world outside.

Paul informed the other three that he wanted to leave, and to release immediately a solo album that he had recorded singlehandedly (give or take a few back-up vocals from Linda) in the Scottish retreat that Jane Asher had advised him to purchase.

There was uproar in the Beatle camp, since Paul's album would have clashed head-on with the last Beatles album, and would have closely followed Ringo's debut solo album, also due to be released at roughly that time. Ringo was accordingly despatched as ambassador to Paul's home in St John's Wood in an attempt to forestall the release of the McCartney album. Paul threw him out, though not before he had impressed upon Ringo his determination to release his own solo album. Ringo thereupon conferred again with the others, and an uneasy compromise was worked out. Ringo's own *Sentimental Journey* was advanced, as was *McCartney*, while the Beatles album was delayed. In the end, there was a fortnight between the release of *Sentimental Journey* and *McCartney*, and three weeks between the latter and *Let It Be*.

But the arrangement had hardly mollified Paul, whose petulent frame of mind was conveyed to the world through a sleeve insert offered with *McCartney*. This took the form of a self-interview. McCartney asked himself questions, and answered them with a succinct directness. In doing so, he shattered any lingering reserves of public hope that the Beatles were still a functioning outfit.

He explained, with a brevity and lack of equivocation that would have been a reporter's dream, that the Beatles were no longer an active group, that he hadn't missed the others in any way, that Allen Klein didn't represent him in any way, and that John's current activities didn't give him any personal pleasure.

All of which was hardly calculated to lead to an early resumption of amicable relations. However, if Paul thought that such a disingenuous tactic would earn him any public affection, he was sadly mistaken. In fact, for someone who had spent his entire professional life smiling at the right moment, exchanging pleasantries as occasion demanded and generally behaving like a P.R. agency's model pupil, it was an astonishingly gauche maneouvre. The self-interview belied the months of frustration he had spent unavailingly trying to keep the group together, and made him seem the force of destruction. Now, while this was clearly intentional, the effect it had was the opposite of the intended one. Instead of Paul appearing as the self-sufficient, composed Beatle, he appeared either sullen and jilted, or complacent and vain, or simply confused. On the one hand, he wanted the music on *McCartney* to express a state of cool-as-a-mountain-stream rural contentment; on the other, the messages that accompanied its release suggested only urban uptightness.

No one thought the music was that good anyway, although hindsight has perhaps allowed its strengths to assume greater prominence. However, what hindsight also reveals is that McCartney's entire solo career could have been predicted with devastating accuracy from just this one album.

What is most apparent is that the songs are half-finished. (Sometimes starkly so: they possess music but no lyrics.) The album could have been a great one had all the songs been fully developed. Now, that doesn't mean that they needed to be coated in sybaritic, Spectorish production techniques. That after all was a relatively late stage in the song-making process; Paul's were deficient because they lacked completeness. His songwriting discipline was exercised only fitfully.

He had always been industrious – often, it could now be seen, to his own creative detriment. Having created a sublime melody, he would move on to produce another,

'Let It Be' – a unique insight into the dissolution of the group

without bothering to ensure that the first had been teased into its proper form. *McCartney* is full of snatches of songs, hummable quatrains that disappear the moment they become interesting. He should have disciplined himself to have created less and perfected more.

Contemporary opinion held that the album contained one indubitable classic – 'Maybe I'm Amazed'; but that was not the only nugget hidden here, as Phoebe Snow demonstrated nine years later when she had a hit single with another track, 'Every Night', and showed just how powerful the song really was when it was tackled with care and thoughtfulness, and not simply tossed aside like a conjuror's last trick. As a songsmith, McCartney had the Midas touch; but he was still sowing his seeds broadcast-style, when he should have been rooting each properly.

Three weeks later, the final Beatles album appeared. "'Get Back', 'Don't Let Me Down' and 12 Other Songs" had long been discarded as a suitable title, since the single it referred to was now over twelve months old. It was unusable in any case, since the combined efforts of the four of them and Phil Spector had not managed to produce the requisite fourteen tracks. There were only ten songs, plus a bit of nothing called 'Dig It', in which Lennon used again the kind of free-form name association he'd employed on 'Give Peace A Chance', and a version of the old Liverpool street song, 'Maggie May', that they hadn't bothered to finish. This was therefore not only the most disappointing Beatles album, but also the shortest, and the most expensive.

Right from the beginning the Beatles had outwitted their contemporaries by the simple device of including seven songs per side as opposed to the standard six. Now, they were forsaking yet more good habits. (And in

cutting the album so short, the Beatles ensured that a wealth of material from those sessions would be left in the can. It seems unlikely that these songs won't, at some point in the distant future, see the light of day.)

It was the most expensive Beatle album because it was marketed as a package with the *Get Back* book, a large format, glossy book of photographs of the filming, with two brief textual passages which were unstructured, unenlightening and horribly (if predictably) sycophantic. Ethan Russell's photographs were exceptionally good, but, those apart, what was the point of it all? Whatever aim the book once had, had long since been forgotten. When it appeared in a boxed package with the album, it just seemed like a gratuitous excuse for charging more for a single album than anybody had ever charged before.

Still, the episode is enlightening on transatlantic differences of opinion. In America, the album was retailed without the book, which has accordingly now become a prized collectors' item there; in Britain, the book was more likely to have been discarded with disgust – it just made it all seem such a shabby and unworthy conclusion.

Let It Be, the album, may have had its merits, but they were well hidden. 'The Long And Winding Road' did indeed sound horrible, but at least that was the only track on which Spector had noticeably overplayed his hand. There were no complaints, for example, about the orchestrations subtly added to John's 'Across The Universe', which now, belatedly, appeared on an official Beatles release.

Nevertheless, what Spector had done was to destroy all semblance of a concept. After all, the album had originally been an attempt to get back to basics, and the fragments that survived to testify to this original intent (for

'John Lennon/Plastic Ono Band', the product of an emotionally ravaged mind

example, there was one track, 'One After 909', a convincing rocker that had been one of the first songs Lennon and McCartney ever composed together; also there were Lennon's closing comments, "I'd like to say thank you very much on behalf of the group and I hope we passed the audition") hardly gelled properly with the kind of full-scale production treatment meted out to 'The Long And Winding Road'. Broken snatches of conversation that had been retained to emphasise the informality of it all just seemed out-of-place.

All in all, the album was a sorry mess, from which no-one emerged with credit; a graceless end to the formal career of the act which had brought a greater degree of visceral change to popular entertainment than anyone since Charles Chaplin.

When the premiere of the *Let It Be* film was held on May 20 1970 none of the Beatles attended. They'd stopped being Beatles. They may further have thought that the film was nothing to be proud of, but in that case they'd have been wrong. Certainly, the film as it finally appeared wickedly mocked the original intention behind it: to show the Beatles as a working band. Instead of that what the public got was a unique documentary insight into the group in the throes of dissolution. No doubt had the movie preceded McCartney's announcement there would have been considerable public perturbation. As it was, the secret was out, the group was no more, and *Let It Be* made fascinating viewing; even in decay, the Beatles were triumphant.

The reason it was so fascinating was that the public was able to glimpse the collapse from the inside for the first time. During the year the four Beatles themselves had virtually disappeared from view. Ringo was sitting in his garden waiting for something to happen; (and, to be fair, composing 'Early 1970'; John

was beginning primal scream therapy; Paul had gone to ground in his Scottish retreat – so successfully that it was during this period that the absurd McCartney-is-dead rumours flourished throughout the U.S. The Apple organisation had managed to restrict the flow of information, so that although the atmosphere between them was known to be disharmonious, no-one had any tangible proof (as opposed to intelligent conjecture) that the end had come. The Beatles had even been unusually fortunate in their press contacts. Ray Connolly, who later wrote the film *That'll Be The Day*, was at that time a reporter on the London *Evening Standard* and was one of those privy to the information that Lennon had left the Beatles – a world exclusive if ever there was one, but Connolly hadn't betrayed Lennon's confidence.

So, after the public had recoiled from what could have been the shock of McCartney's announcement, *Let It Be* gave them an opportunity to put the events of the last eighteeen months into clear perspective. It made a sorry end to a squalid chapter. "Would the Rolling Stones ever break up?" a member of the press asked Mick Jagger, "Nah," he replied, "and if we did we wouldn't be so bitchy about it."

The other three hadn't been given much advance warning of Paul's intentions of going public; they hadn't known he was going to spill the beans, and they certainly hadn't known he was going to do it in the clumsy way he chose. So Paul had fixed the timing himself, and he was the one with the new solo album release able to take advantage of the situation. However, if he was a bit smug about his own future prospects, in comparison with those of the others, he was quickly shaken from his conceit by the uncertain reception given to *McCartney*.

Paul's actions had proved most embarrass-

After 'Sentimental Journey' and 'Beaucoups of Blues', Ringo busied himself in the film industry.

ing for Ringo, who was in the doldrums after committing what was now seen to be a grievous *faux pas* with *Sentimental Journey*. This was because the release of the album coincided with all the publicity concerning the break-up – making it seem as though the album was Ringo's quick-fire entry in the solo stakes. This was not the case at all. He had conceived it as an off-the-wall enterprise to which no particular significance would be attached. That much can be said in Ringo's defence. Because *Sentimental Journey* was one of those projects that begged failure: an album of hoary popular standards that he had apparently recorded for his mother. It's hard to imagine a voice less suited than Ringo's to the task of crooning Sinatra-style through schmaltzy fare like 'Love Is A Many Splendoured Thing'.

Actually, even if Ringo had sung them all perfectly, the album would still have been a retrograde step because the Beatles were the ones who had revolutionised popular music, by providing new criteria and a fresh set of classics. They had pulled the rug from underneath sentimental songs like those Ringo was now covering.

Ringo's filming activities hadn't been dazzingly successful, either. He'd had a small part in *Candy*, but it was *The Magic Christian*, in which he co-starred with Peter Sellers, which was felt to offer the best opportunity for him to show whether or not he was going to make headway in the movies. The end result was not encouraging. He didn't manage to produce a credible characterisation and the film itself, unfortunately like many of Sellers' efforts, was funny in places and disappointing in toto.

Mostly, however, Ringo was keen to atone for *Sentimental Journey*. The opportunity arose very quickly, when he met Pete Drake while both of them were working on Harrison's *All Things Must Pass*. Drake had worked with Bob Dylan on *Nashville Skyline*, and on Dylan's recommendation had been invited over to London by Harrison to add his distinctive steel guitar to tracks like 'The Ballad Of Sir Frankie Crisp'. Ringo mentioned to Drake, just by way of conversation, that he was interested in doing a country album.

Drake took him at his word, and fixed it all up. He was one of the foremost Nashville cats, with a formidable reputation, so in no time at all he had arranged studio facilities, first-class session musicians and a fistful of previously unrecorded country songs which he'd obtained from the catalogues of local publishers. All Ringo had to do was to fly in and sing naturally. Drake said the whole thing would be completed in two days, though in the event it took six. Surely no Beatle had ever had it that easy before, at least not since the days when they had been deferential to George Martin. They're all nine-to-fivers in Nashville (which is not to denigrate their manifold talents) and it must all have seemed like the complete reverse of the standard anarchic Beatles recording session.

Ringo took his chance well, and his homely lugubrious voice suited those typically maudlin country songs like a charm. It's one of the best Beatle solo albums.

Unfortunately for Ringo however, Beatle fans had already gone out en masse to purchase *Sentimental Journey* (in America, particularly), and they were not amused. Hence when *Beaucoups Of Blues* appeared but a few months later they were exceedingly wary, and the album registered very disappointing sales. In the U.K., of course, he had not expected to do as well, since country music had never then enjoyed wide popularity.

It was a very disappointing business. Ringo became disillusioned and restricted his recording activities to occasional singles during the early '70s. He busied himself in the film industry, and took a rest from albums. He should have returned to Nashville and put together another country record. It's something he should still do today.

The entire *Beaucoups Of Blues* album was probably completed more quickly than any one of the tracks on *All Things Must Pass*, the triple album with which George Harrison launched his solo career.

Whereas the timing of the end of the Beatles had inconvenienced Ringo, so that his solo career had started almost by default, it could not have been more propitious for George. His own stature as an individual performer had been growing steadily, both through his compositions, especially the *Abbey Road* pair, 'Something' and 'Here Comes The Sun'. There was also his close friendship with Eric Clapton; the two had written and recorded 'Badge' together, one of the best singles to come from Clapton's group, Cream. They had also espoused and popularised U.S. rock acts – not only Delaney and Bonnie, but also The Band.

All in all, Harrison's credibility was building to a peak. Even as the last rites were being performed over the Beatles at the premiere of *Let It Be*, he was moving into Apple studios to begin recording his own material, having commandeered Phil Spector to act as co-producer; Harrison had no complaints about the *Let It Be* album. (Indeed, he'd had his usual quota of two songs which, given that there were fewer tracks this time, was his highest percentage score to date!)

Apparently, they thought there was enough material for an album when they went into the studios, but things went very well so they decided to make it a double, and then things went fantastically well, so it somehow

became a treble, rock music's first. In view of this it's not surprising that the sessions took as long as they did – nearly six months.

Fashions change, in rock more than in most other fields, and today *All Things Must Pass* tends to be derided. Its time will undoubtedly come again, for much of the work is excellent. Harrison's artistic development had been both fostered and stunted by working in close proximity to Lennon and McCartney: fostered because the competitive atmosphere encouraged him to write his own songs, and stunted because he was frequently not given chance to display his emerging talents. This had been a source of rancour towards the end, but by now George probably recognised that it put him in a strong position. Free of all restrictions, he was able to formulate his own album, and he had several unrecorded songs of high quality readily available.

'My Sweet Lord' was the album's outstanding track, and its extraordinary success as a single was the foundation on which the album's unprecedented sales were built (an immensely rewarding situation for George at the time, but one which was to cause him headaches later on).

'Awaiting On You All', 'Isn't It A Pity' (of which there were two versions) and 'What Is Life' were also all excellent songs. If attractive melodies seemed to be in abundance, then equally George had no problems with lyrical subject-matter. There were songs about his Friar Park home, built by the eccentric Sir Frankie Crisp, and about the Apple scruffs, the girls who kept permanent vigil in the street outside the Beatles offices. When George had completed the song, he invited them inside to hear it.

The album also had the benefit of a new song Harrison had co-written with Bob Dylan, 'I'd Have You Anytime', and there

was also a version of 'If Not For You', from Dylan's *New Morning*.

Many of the top instrumentalists of the day contributed to the work, including Jim Gordon (drums), Carl Radle (bass) and Bobby Whitlock (keyboards), all of whom were shortly to set up shop with Eric Clapton as Derek and the Dominoes; Clapton was the album's most surprising absentee.

The production was excellent, retaining the wide-screen qualities which most distinguished Spector's work, while allowing particular instruments to break through when necessary.

Harrison, like Lennon at this stage, seemed to tape everything in the belief that it must be of public interest, and so the final two sides of the album consisted of studio jamming sessions, when the musicians had been idly, as they thought, enjoying themselves. This music comprised the third album, which was meant to be free, but, as usual,

only tended to make the first two unusually expensive. There were some adverse comments about this particular device, but otherwise the album was warmly welcomed by both critics and public; a hit, a palpable hit. Far from being overshadowed in the Beatle solo stakes by the two main songwriters in the group, Harrison had emerged as the most impressive of them all. The album sold more than *McCartney* and *John Lennon/ Plastic Ono Band* put together.

The dawning of a new decade does not usually make any great difference to the way people lead their lives. Some might use the occasion to make determined resolutions, but there would be few who could subsequently claim that the time had represented a watershed in their lives.

John Lennon would have been one, though. From January 1970 his life seemed to change completely, a change he symbolised by having his hair cut in Denmark at the end of December 1969. Both he and Yoko (she'd had hers cut too) subsequently donated their shorn locks to Michael X's Blackhouse, which was founded with the intention of becoming a centre for black culture in Islington, North London. (Michael X – Michael Abdul Malik – was later hanged on murder charges in the West Indies, and thus the Lennons' generosity towards him, since they had made financial as well as tonsorial contributions to his cause, made them seem very gullible; but at least they did not behave with animosity towards him after he'd betrayed their trust, and in fact they were the only ones to send funds to contribute towards his defence costs at the end.)

Apart from recording 'Instant Karma', Lennon did little. After the almost non-stop activities of the previous year, he needed to recharge his batteries. John and Yoko did not venture much from their Tittenhurst Park home. In fact, they did not venture much from the bedroom of their Tittenhurst Park home . . . The time spent in isolation did, however, begin to put a strain on their relationship.

In April Paul McCartney phoned him to say that he too was leaving the Beatles and putting out a solo album. Though this matter should by now have been of little importance to Lennon, it did intensify his sadness of that period. Anthony Fawcett, in *John Lennon: One Day At A Time*, says, "The next morning when John saw the headlines in all the daily papers that Paul had quit the Beatles to put out his own record, he felt a twinge of bitterness. Here was Paul making an 'event' out of leaving the group, doing exactly what he had pleaded with John not to do just six months before.

"John was confused, even though he had wanted the break-up so badly, now that it had happened the emotional intensity of the Beatles' end hit him hard."

By this time, John and Yoko had already become involved with primal therapy, after a Californian psychologist, Arthur Janov, had mailed his book *The Primal Scream* direct to their home. It would be mischievous to suggest that this had been a long-shot publicity exercise; but if it had been, the results could hardly have been more fruitful. Within months most of the Western world had heard of primal screams.

The essence of primal therapy is that children repress their own emotions, almost from birth. After being frustrated in their attempts to obtain unbounded parental love, they inevitably build up defence mechanisms to protect them from the pain of being unloved. Such defences are carried with them for the rest of their lives. In other words, people are only able to survive through having learned how to suppress their innermost emotions, and consequently the human being stops feeling the pain they cause. However, there is a price to pay, and that is tension and neurosis, as real emotions always remain unfulfilled, and therefore a state of psychological equilibrium becomes impossible to attain. Therefore it is only by going back to childhood, back through all the defences, and breaking through the primal barrier (an experience which is inevitably painful, and induces primal screams in the patients) that one can discover one's real needs and become a real person again.

That's the theory, and Lennon warmed to it straightaway – not unsurprisingly, since he had had to repress a great deal of his own childhood. However, he was becoming aware himself that his automatic espousal of anything new, whether it was people or ideas or both (he was what Christopher Booker might have termed a neophiliac), did not always have a beneficial outcome. He'd been duped by too many psychic medicine men. Nevertheless, Yoko's reading of the book confirmed his own favourable impression, and so after a few transatlantic phone calls, Janov himself arrived at the Lennons' home to initiate them into primal therapy.

It was during this first course of treatment that Lennon last saw Cynthia. Janov had told John that one of the reasons why he was feeling neurotic was that he was guilty about having deprived his son of paternal attention since having become involved with Yoko. John therefore set about remedying this, and immediately contacted Cynthia and announced that he was coming round. There was a happy family reunion, which was interrupted by a phone call from Tittenhurst Park to inform them that Yoko had taken an overdose. She had tried to commit suicide once before in Japan when one of her first 'events' had been heavily criticised; now she was distraught that John had returned to his family. He rushed back to Yoko, and never saw Cynthia again.

Janov spent three weeks in England with the Lennons, but suggested that for the therapy to be completely successful they would need to attend his Californian clinic for intensive treatment over a four-month period. And so they did. The difficulties over John's U.S. entry permit were waived, and they completed their primal treatment. Afterwards they returned to England, each to record albums which showed the results of primal therapy.

The Lennon album – *John Lennon/Plastic Ono Band* – certainly seemed the product of an emotionally ravaged mind. John was doing in public what Janov had taught him to do in private – to uncover all the bitterness and anxieties of his life, so that he could face up to them, and in doing so get back to his true self. It may have been a psychologically harrowing album, but it worked because the desperate honesty of the performance overwhelmed the listener.

The album had been co-produced by Phil Spector, an assignment he handled virtually concurrently with George's *All Things Must Pass*, and the two works could not have been more dissimilar. George's was lavish, with some sweeping arrangements and a studio full of session players, while John's was ascetic and stripped down to what was absolutely basic (a bit like a Samuel Becket play, or Ernest Hemingway's *The Old Man And The Sea*). John needed to make only two phone calls to obtain his complement of musicians: while he played guitar and piano, Ringo was on drums and Klaus Voormann on bass. (Also, Billy Preston did play keyboards on one track.)

There was a second distinction. George was writing songs that either had their roots in aspects of the Beatle legend ('Apple Scruffs'),

or else re-affirmed the dogmas, the Eastern mysticism that had been interwoven with the final days of the group.

John's album swept away all that in an orgy of iconoclasm. He uprooted the Beatle citadel, trying to expunge every trace of it. It was important that in doing so he spoke plainly, without metaphor and in simple direct language. There was no room for ambiguity this time, and this was the only way in which he could possibly have attempted the de-mystification of the Beatles.

Lennon had felt more than the others the awful predicament of the group once they had become not simply pop stars, but the artistic gurus of a generation. Somehow they had lost sight of rock 'n' roll and their original metier. They tried to get it back, and to renounce their status as demi-gods, but it was like escaping from quicksand; even as they attempted to extricate themselves, so they were sucked further in. Attempts to debunk the Beatles myth only intensified the hero worship, since, as rock stars, their very mastery of the medium led them inevitably to greater sophistication and artistry.

This contradiction is seen most clearly on the White Album. On the one hand, Lennon tries to undermine the fanaticism of their fervid following by turning out lyrics that are deliberately meaningless (*"A soap impression of his wife/Which he ate and donated to the National Trust"*), but on the other hand they rejected George Martin's advice to strip the double-album to a single one, containing only straightforward songs, so that they could include tracks like 'Revolution No. 9', the most conceited attempt at 'artistry' there had been in ages. They said they wanted to be honest-to-goodness rock stars, and not 'significant artists', but the lure of the latter proved difficult to resist. The Beatles, and especially Lennon, had not managed to be completely honest with either themselves or their audience. So with *John Lennon/Plastic Ono Band*, Lennon was screaming honesty with stark simplicity; standing emotionally naked, with nothing up his sleeve.

Even now, though, there was a slight, albeit forgiveable, contradiction. Lennon was trampling into the ground the Beatles and everything they had ever stood for; putting the group's entire history into the shredder, so that he could emerge completely free, as a new man and a new artiste. What he could never overcome was that the very thing that made that process so fascinating to millions was the fact that it had been made by John Lennon, ex-Beatle. Had it been made by John Lennon, ex-Quarry Bank schoolboy, very few would have been interested.

The legend was a Hydra, and Lennon was never going to defeat it.

CHAPTER
4

Out On Their Own

Throughout most of the '70s, lawyers working on behalf of the Beatles were incessantly engaged on litigation of some kind. The whole weary, and expensive, process was set in train by Paul McCartney in December 1970 when he initiated high court proceedings to dissolve the Beatles' partnership. He had wanted to sue Allen Klein, who was holding him to his obligations under an old contract; effectively, he was acting as Paul's manager even though Paul had never consented (indeed, had adamantly rejected) such an arrangement. However, the only way he was able to sue Klein was by suing Apple and John, George and Ringo, and it was his understandable reluctance to do this that had delayed proceedings until the end of the year.

It must be remembered that, despite everything that had happened during the '60s, once the Beatles had ceased to be, the four as individuals found they had very little money coming in. All their finances were channelled through the Beatles' partnership and Apple (and, therefore, Allen Klein). In March 1971 a receiver was appointed to handle the

Beatles' assets, and Klein was excluded from further management of the group's affairs. The effect of this, however, was simply to freeze the Beatles' common funds for some time.

In June 1973 the saga took a new turn, when Paul's estimation of Klein as a "trained New York crook" was belatedly accepted by the others. John, George, Ringo, Yoko and Apple started an action against Klein and his ABKCO company. They alleged that ABKCO and Klein took excessive commissions, practised fraud, suggested conduct which would have been a fraud on the tax authorities of the U.S. and U.K., mismanaged Bangla Desh, and otherwise mismanaged the group's affairs.

Characteristically, Klein retaliated, suing John, George, Ringo, Yoko and Apple for damages of $63,461,372.87, plus future earnings. He also brought an action against Paul, alleging conspiracy with the others "wantonly, maliciously, fraudulently, wrongfully and intentionally without justification in law or fact to damage or injure plaintiff." Damages

22nd February, 1971. Paul goes to Court to have the Beatle partnership dissolved. His Counsel alleged that Klein could not be trusted with the stewardship of the group's assets.

were sought for this alleged conspiracy of $34 million, plus interest. In the end, Klein didn't do badly, receiving about $5 million, the price the Beatles had to pay to be rid of him.

The Beatles' final legal and financial dissolution occurred in January 1975. It was only after that that the four as solo artistes received individual payment for their solo efforts.

The sue-you-sue-me blues didn't stop there, however. As late as May 1979, Apple were still issuing writs, filing an £8 million claim against Capitol Records, alleging non-payment of royalties.

Of the four Beatles, John and George, for their different reasons, had felt the more frustrated within the group, and they therefore felt the keener sense of relief when it had all been concluded (however messily). Hardly surprisingly, it was they who derived most immediate benefit, with excellent albums on sale before the end of the year in which the group had fractured.

Ringo and Paul reacted differently; in their cases, the effect was shattering. They'd been the two eager to keep the show on the road, and hence they were the ones initially disoriented by its demise. They were not able to attain a creative plateau of their own for some considerable time. This, however, may have been no bad thing. Even at this early stage, both Lennon and Harrison had already painted themselves into corners.

John Lennon/Plastic Ono Band had been effectively cathartic album in the way that John's current guru, Arthur Janov, must have intended. John had flushed out his soul, simultaneously expunging both the myth of the Beatles and the enormous psychological burden that was its legacy; the mental wear-and-tear of those years must have been incalculable. The only problem was this: if Lennon had successfully undergone such

Ringo dispels intimations of inadequacy with 'It Don't Come Easy'

spiritual cleansing, then surely his future work should have been free of the emotional shackles of the past. This proved not to be the case.

George's problem was simple. In choosing to issue a triple-album so quickly, he had put all his eggs in one basket. The condition itself was not uncommon among artistes. Joseph Heller had enjoyed so much success with his first novel, *Catch-22*, that it took him eighteen years to write another. George similarly seemed to have given all he'd got straightaway, and in doing so exhausted both the potential of the individual style he had developed, and also his own immediate reserves of creativity. Nicholas Schaffner has pointed out that both Lennon and Harrison thus landed themselves at artistic dead-ends. "Both ex-Beatles would find it difficult either to duplicate their considerable achievements, or to establish a convincing new direction."

For the moment, each had nevertheless done more than enough to justify his stature as a solo artiste. Paul had not yet come up to expectations, but no one doubted his capacity, in time, to do so. The burden of proving an individual virility therefore fell most heavily upon Ringo.

By the early months of 1971, he was feeling distinctly uneasy. George's 'My Sweet Lord' had just spent five weeks throughout January and February holding down the No. 1 spot, and in March Paul's 'Another Day' had swept effortlessly to No. 2. Ringo was thus suddenly left as the only Beatle not to have made his own impression upon the Top 20.

In fact, he did already have the answer in 'It Don't Come Easy', a song he had recorded in February 1970 with Klaus Voorman, Stephen Stills and George Harrison, who also acted as producer. 'It Don't Come Easy': what a wealth of information the title betrays. Ringo had written the song himself in the group's final days, when his personal future seemed full of uncertainty. The song was presumably indicative of the pressure he felt to deliver something of his own, and of the fact that he didn't feel himself naturally suited to the task. Under such circumstances the title, presumably, did come easy.

The b-side, 'Early 1970', also reflected Ringo's unease. Here, Ringo had written a verse for each member of the group, revealing that while George was still actively supporting him, Paul and John were each too tied up in domestic affairs to bother. And Ringo, who delimited his own musical prowess in the last verse, clearly needed the support of all three.

Self-pitying, perhaps, but it was also a little touching and showed that, if anything, Ringo had become the victim of his own image. As it turned out, he was certainly underestimating himself. 'It Don't Come Easy' was a triumphant success, outselling singles from the other three that were issued during that period ('Another Day', 'Power To The People' and 'Bangla Desh', from Paul, John and George respectively), and acting like a white tornado in dispelling Ringo's intimations of inadequacy. It did wonders both for his self-esteem and his bank balance.

Lennon's 'Power To The People', released in March, was a drab affair. One again, he'd chosen to construct a song from the simple foundation of a political slogan. This time, however, it was not one of his own, but a particularly well-used, largely meaningless, expression. Lennon set it to music better than anyone else could have done, but that is not to say that it was effective; the music lacked the beautiful simplicity of 'Give Peace A Chance', and the lyrics, however well-intentioned, were trite. No artiste can afford to subordinate his own creativity to a political orthodoxy of the day, and with 'Power To The People', Lennon was entering

While John tapped the raw commitment of the militant underprivileged, Paul catered for the bourgeois sensibilities of the drawing-room

a long, dark tunnel. If the single itself wasn't sufficient evidence of this, the accompanying publicity material, showing the Lennons in military-style revolutionary garb, was. If, as he was to state on *Imagine*, John didn't want to be a soldier, why was he dressing up like one?

'Another Day', Paul McCartney's debut solo single, was as far away from 'Power to The People' as it is possible to get. If the latter was blithe propaganda for the masses, 'Another Day' was closely-observed domesticity, a song, in the noble tradition of 'Eleanor Rigby', about a lonely woman. While John was tapping and reinforcing the raw commitment of the militant under-privileged, Paul was catering for the bourgeois sensibilities of the drawing-room. The gulf between the two halves of the most productive songwriting partnership of the century could never have been better illustrated.

Although 'Another Day' has been the subject of much critical disparagement as the composition which first evinced the concern for humdrum, homely values that was to characterise McCartney's work thereafter, that assessment leaves several factors out of consideration. 'Another Day' was slight and simple, but it did have a delicate charm, and displayed attributes which Paul could have profitably developed. For one thing, it is well constructed, and for another it strives to present a realistic character portrait. The song is disciplined, and it relates to real life. These were positive qualities, the staple of the best popular music, and yet Paul discarded them almost straightaway. It's just possible that it was the lukewarm critical reception given to 'Another Day' that pushed Paul into difficulties, rather than out of them, because *Ram* is so terrible it's hard to know where to begin.

There isn't a single consistently effective track on the album. Traces of melody can occasionally be perceived, surfacing for air in the ocean of mediocrity, and reminding us all that at his best McCartney has few peers in the art of music-making; but they are never intelligently developed. Worse, the lyrics are hopelessly inept, totally devoid of wit or real purpose. On the evidence of *Ram* alone, one would have to conclude that McCartney lacked all sense of humour. Since that was a conclusion that could hardly be countenanced, it must simply have been that at this time McCartney had an over-serious estimation of his own worth. The touch of humility that should have reminded him that he was subject to the same laws as all other men had temporarily gone AWOL. Really, it was *Magical Mystery Tour* all over again, except that this time McCartney did not have even the other three to share his worst embarrassments, or the excuse that he was working in an unfamiliar medium.

In fact, Paul served himself badly as songwriter and appallingly as producer. He clearly lacked the guidance of someone to explain how to nurture the foetal compositions into full-blooded life. All the tracks are messy, and invariably either too brief or over-long. Some change course half-way through, or display less glaring signs of schizophrenia. The syndrome is epitomised by a strangely distended track called 'Long Haired Lady', which has several diverse parts, two of which feature decent tunes trying to get out. Similarly, 'The Back Seat Of My Car' has a couple of good refrains that assert their independence amidst the overall confusion.

McCartney, through George Martin, had become acquainted with the range of studio trickery that can be utilised to give colour, range and form to a song; but he seems to have become so obsessed with the possibilities thus offered that he'd blinded himself to the most crucial factor – the quality of the song itself.

In any case, it was particularly disappointing when McCartney could do no more than recall past triumphs – as, for example, during 'Uncle Albert/Admiral Halsey', when the background effects recall those used on 'Yellow Submarine'. (Other parts of the track bring to mind the Bonzo Dog Band, whom McCartney had on one occasion produced.)

However bad it was, at least one person saw it as a challenge. John Lennon was listening closely. *Ram* virtually opened with the line *"Too many people going underground . . .",* and on the evidence of lines like that, a song called '3 Legs' and other scattered references, John gathered that Paul was casting aspersions on his career, and his new and passionate commitment to political action. If his line of thought hadn't been influenced by the lyrics, it would have been determined by the crude pictures on the back cover, which showed, in quite unambiguous detail, one Beetle fucking another. (Perhaps after all Paul had lost his sense of humour.) John was to waste little time in taking up the cudgels.

In the meantime, *Ram* was universally condemned. It was pilloried as the moment of true Beatle nemesis. *Rolling Stone* referred to it as "the nadir in the decomposition of '60s rock thus far", describing it as "incredibly inconsequential" and "monumentally irrelevant". McCartney, who'd made the album in New York and had intended it to be a more lavish and professional effort to contrast with the ascetic, homespun atmosphere of *McCartney*, was shocked, mystified and resentful.

The summer of 1971 was a lively and decisive period for three of the ex-Beatles. Paul may have temporarily retired hurt, but the others were busy. Ringo, buoyant after the global success of 'It Don't Come Easy',

happily returned to filming, taking up an intriguing opportunity to play Frank Zappa in Frank Zappa's own film, *200 Motels* and then moving on to Spain to film *Blindman*. John was working on *Imagine*, which he intended to make into both an album and a film. George was involved in the complex arrangements for the Bangla Desh concert.

The refugee problem of Bangla Desh developed swiftly and tragically during the spring and summer months of 1971. The area was the eastern half of Pakistan, the country that had been created rather artificially in two distinct halves at the time of Indian independence, because it combined the Muslim territories on India's northern flanks. The Bengali-speaking peoples of the eastern sector were persecuted by the military rulers of West Pakistan in response to an attempt to assert their democratic rights, coupled with – when that approach proved fruitless – an attempt to secede from the union altogether. Brutal suppression by the military authorities, combined with the disease, poverty and frequently inhospitable climatic conditions that are endemic in the region, created an appalling refugee problem, with millions pouring across the border into India, a country whose own problems in feeding its inhabitants hardly qualified it to deal capably with a sudden population inflow. The ensuing chaos and human suffering was quickly highlighted by the world's press and television.

Ravi Shankar, a Bengali himself, was naturally concerned with the plight of his fellow countrymen. He relayed his thoughts to George Harrison, with whom he was then collaborating on the soundtrack of *Raga* (a film which was primarily devoted to Shankar, but which did include some interesting footage of Harrison being taught to play the sitar). George said he'd do what he could to help.

What George did was to organise the greatest indoor rock concert ever. Pictured here with sitar maestro, Ravi Shankar.

What he did was to organise the greatest indoor rock concert that had ever taken place. With very little time for preparation, he booked Madison Square Garden in New York, and arranged two concerts there on August 1 1971. He managed to enlist the aid of several close friends: Ringo was lured away from his filming activities in Spain; Eric Clapton and Leon Russell both agreed to appear; there were many others whose participation one might have expected since they were associated with the Apple stable of artists: Billy Preston, Badfinger and Klaus Voorman. In addition, many top session musicians – Jesse Ed Davis, Chuck Findlay, Jim Keltner, Jim Horn, Carl Radle, *et al* – enthusiastically responded to George's request for volunteers.

So did John Lennon. His Toronto appearance in 1969 had re-kindled his appetite for stage work – not that one would have guessed as much, so irregular were his appearances. However, he was willing to help George in what seemed destined to be a major occasion, and so, having wrapped up work on *Imagine*, he and Yoko flew to New York.

He would have increased the ex-Beatle turn-out to 75%, but for an argument that developed between him and George. John was assuming that he would be appearing on stage with Yoko; George was adamant that Yoko had not been invited, and that there was no room for her. John was upset, especially since Yoko scolded him for not having presented her case more forcibly to George. He resolved his difficulty characteristically, simply by flying straight back to England; he didn't even wait for Yoko, who was left behind to sort out a few arrangements and follow him.

The incident was a typical one in the history of the Beatles. Firstly, it was vaguely unpleasant, and secondly, the unpleasantness was largely unnecessary. Ever since Yoko had appeared in the studio during the recording of the 'White Album', there had been resentment at her intrusion. In this particular case, it is clearly sad that there was no-one around who could intercede and work out an arrangement satisfactory to both parties. In the absence of such a person, however, it is hard not to sympathise with George. Yoko's musical contributions of this period tended to be not only free-form, but also somewhat self-indulgent, an aurally taxing experience for even the most obliging audience. George had in any case already arranged a lengthy opening contribution from Ravi Shankar, and it was uncertain how the audience would react to that. Also, of course, with many top-name guests having already consented to appear, there was clearly a lot to fit in. After all, even Eric Clapton didn't get a solo spot.

There had never been a real possibility that the Beatles might reunite for the Bangla Desh benefit, even though both George and Ringo performed, and John almost did. Some years later Paul told *Rolling Stone*, "George invited me, and I must say it was more than just visa problems. At the time there was the whole Apple thing. When the Beatles broke up, at first I thought, 'Right, broken up, no more messing with any of that.' George came up and asked if I wanted to play Bangla Desh, and I thought, blimey, what's the point? We've just broken up and we're joining up again? It just seemed a bit crazy.

"There were a lot of things that went down then, most of which I've forgotten now. I really felt annoyed – 'I'm not going to do that if he won't bloody let me out of my contract.'

"It was a little tit-for-tat, if you're not going to do this for me, I'm not going to do that for you."

At the centre of this disagreement was, of course, Allen Klein, since it was he that Paul was really fighting, and not the other three. However, there is little doubt that Paul's attitude suited him marvellously. Klein wanted to be holding the reins of this vast and prestigious charitable occasion, with McCartney strictly on the outside. The more McCartney could be painted as a peevish, selfish individual, the better Klein liked it.

The converse of this is, of course, that had there been a less inflexible personality than Klein in charge of proceedings, it is highly likely that a reunion would have taken place. This is admittedly pure speculation, but Klein did want McCartney separated from the others; had someone in his position ardently wanted a reunion, it is perfectly likely that he could have engineered one, since in reality there was very little that prevented either John or Paul from attending the concert.

George would not have been party to these machinations. Nevertheless, with Paul's attendance ruled out, clearly there would be no Beatles reunion, hence George was not obliged to meet Yoko's demands. In any case, he probably sensed that, had John and Yoko appeared, they would have monopolised the attention of the media; George, who had masterminded the whole event, understandably wanted it to be known that it was he who was running this show.

In the event, the non-appearance of John and Yoko was virtually irrelevant, so impressive was the cast-list. Over the days preceding the concerts, there had been a swell of anticipation throughout New York, with wild rumours circulating about just who might be appearing. There had been no leaks of advance information either to substantiate

The subsequent duplicity and financial shenanigans never detracted from the mythic qualities of Bangla Desh.

or confirm these rumours, and in most circumstances it is likely that the concert-goers would simply have been disappointed. The Concert for Bangla Desh was an exception; one of the few occasions in Beatle history when wild rumours about intended activities were not disappointed by events.

Harrison introduced Shankar, who opened the concert, and then appeared himself fronting the all-star rock orchestra whose principle players have already been mentioned. Half-way through some already memorable proceedings, he calmly played his master-stroke, by bringing on to the stage Bob Dylan.

Although Dylan had appeared at the 1969 Isle of Wight festival, it had been some years since he had played in America, and his presence transformed the occasion from a very memorable one into one of the truly outstanding events in the history of rock 'n' roll. As people immediately pointed out, it was the first time that Dylan and any of the Beatles had ever appeared on stage together. The concerts, of course, had sold out virtually as soon as they were announced; Dylan's presence ensured that the proceeds from the ancillary projects planned – a film and album of the event – would be spectacular.

The appearance of Dylan was also welcome because his own career had been in some difficulties. He had released two albums in 1970 – one, *Self-Portrait*, disastrous, and the other, *New Morning*, acceptable without being fired with Dylan's past commitment. When he re-appeared at Madison Square Garden, the public were overjoyed to note that it seemed once again to be the Dylan of old – playing the songs, and dressing the part, of the pre-motorcycle accident days. It must have been a restorative moment for Dylan himself. No doubt he was pleased to have participated. He attended Patti Harrison's post-gig party, and later used concert photographs for the sleeve of his next album release, *More Bob Dylan Greatest Hits*.

In every other possible way, the concerts were an unqualified success. Musically, Harrison had assembled together many of the top names of the day, who had all delivered good performances on the night, even though there had been only one full day available for rehearsals, and who had all behaved with perfect equanimity (the contretemps with Lennon was not public knowledge, of course). Everything ran smoothly, because everything had been organised properly – once again, despite the absence of time for preparation. Finally, the concerts showed emphatically that popular music, which the Beatles had transformed into a highly lucrative, global industry, did have its philanthropic aspect. After the débâcle of the Rolling Stones' Altamont concert, and the atmosphere of despair thereafter (the deaths of Janis Joplin, Jim Morrison and Jimi Hendrix, and the break-up of the Beatles), it was like a rediscovery of faith. Harrison had put rock music back on course.

The subsequent duplicity and financial shenanigans never detracted from the mythic qualities of the event itself. Since they were outside the control of the artistes themselves, that is fair enough. It is certainly true, however, that future promoters of charity concerts would have learned much from the Bangla Desh experiences, had they familiarised themselves with the facts of the case.

Basically, the facts were that only a proportion of the funds that had been raised ever reached Bangla Desh, and that those that did arrive took an age in getting there.

There were a variety of reasons for this. Whether or not the involvement of Allen Klein was a major or minor factor will perhaps never be clear. Some months after the Bangla Desh concerts, an article in *New York* magazine alleged that monies from the enterprise had been diverted into Klein's own bank account. Klein, the epitome of outraged innocence, responded in characteristically extravagant style with a $100,000,000 lawsuit. He has never pursued this, however, and in the wake of his 1979 prison sentence for income tax fraud at the time of his association with the Beatles, it's unlikely that he ever will.

Klein may have been a considerable handicap to the prompt and honourable disbursal of the Bangla Desh funds, but he was by no means the only one.

Various record companies entered the lists, claiming, quite justifiably, to have particular artistes under exclusive contract. Unfortunately, there had been insufficient legal preparation for the concert. Many artistes had not signed contractual releases ensuring their right to play – or, more importantly, to be featured as part of the follow-up projects. Since CBS were one of the aggrieved organisations, and since Bob Dylan, whose presence in the spin-off projects was clearly vital, was one of their artistes, this was a wrangle that had to be resolved. Some companies had a secondary, complaint, inferring that the release of the Bangla Desh concert album would damage the sales of already-scheduled releases by artistes of theirs who had participated in it.

Further problems were caused simply because the recording appeared on the Apple label, since by then the company was under siege from lawyers, accountants and sundry other financial advisers. A further difficulty was experienced because Klein tried to negotiate one-off distribution deals, ostensibly on the grounds that he was attempting to minimise the otherwise exorbitant retail price of a triple-album. (In Britain, the album was distributed by CBS; Apple product was customarily handled by EMI). It was a result of these assorted problems that the release of the album was delayed until early the following year, something which in itself fomented rumours of financial wheeler-dealing.

Thus in the end the album-of-the-concert arrived only a few months before the film-of-the-concert. The movie, directed by Saul Swimmer, proved to be an entertaining and well-recorded memorial of the event. There were few precedents (other than *Woodstock*) for a live rock concert for spawning both an album and a film. The three-way concept brought rich dividends. A cheque was donated to UNICEF straightaway for $243,418 – the proceeds of the concerts themselves. The album and film together were estimated to have raised a further $10,000,000. Even after this money had surmounted all the hazards outlined above, however, it still did not find its way to Bangla Desh for many years, since it fell foul of a more conventional fiscal hurdle – the U.S. Internal Revenue Service.

However sordid the financial manoeuverings, and however sour the after-taste, the concert itself had been a huge success, the gesture magnanimous, and the overall concept enterprising. George Harrison was quite rightly singled out as the man deserving all the praise, and his reputation stood higher even than it had at the time of *All Things Must Pass*. With him as the new torch-bearer, the Beatles still seemed possessed of refulgent properties.

Subsequently, the Concert for Bangla Desh came to represent a watershed. The stock of the individual Beatles was then at its highest, as though they were enjoying a post-split honeymoon, with John, Ringo and George already having distinguished themselves. For his part, Paul had enjoyed predictable commercial success, if little critical favour. He may have found the criticism displeasing, but it was not intended maliciously; it was just that *McCartney* had its faults, and *Ram* had more.

Up to this point, the individual Beatles still enjoyed the unswerving loyalty and devotion of fans the world over, just as they had done in group days. The Beatles, whether all for one or all for each other, still towered over the rock establishment, supreme and invulnerable.

CHAPTER 5

Come Together

Returning to England after his abortive Bangla Desh appearance, John engaged once more in desultory political activities. He joined a protest march against internment in Northern Ireland, and donated £1000 to the fighting fund for the Upper Clyde Shipbuilders, an industrial issue which at that time had become the focus of left-wing antipathy towards Edward Heath's Conservative government. Shortly after that he and Yoko left the country, resuming their constantly interrupted search for Yoko's young daughter, Kyoko; she was forever disappearing in company with her father, Anthony Cox, Yoko's second husband (John was her third). Cox was an American film producer, who seemed to have produced little other than Yoko's films.

John and Yoko went briefly, futilely, to the Virgin Islands, and then moved on to New York. To begin with, they stayed at the St Regis Hotel, before renting a studio in Greenwich Village. In 1973 they purchased the first of their apartments in the Dakota block.

Lennon never returned to Britain. Certainly, he had never consciously intended to leave, and possessions from his magnificient Tittenhurst Park estate (which he sold to Ringo) were gradually shipped out to New York.

The complete change seemed to suit him, though. For the moment, he had exhausted the possibilities offered by England; not surprisingly, for his most abiding characteristic was his constant, desperate search for new stimuli. Ideas appealed to him by virtue of their novelty, and anybody who seemed to have anything new to offer (Magic Alex, the Maharishi, Arthur Janov, *et al*) became instantly a source of fascination. The converse, of course, was inevitably true. Lennon became easily bored, and then he reacted simply by casting aside whatever it was that had ceased to amuse him. In this case, it was England.

There were positive pleasures in moving to America: he relished the pace and energy of life in 24-hour New York. He said that he had always felt a child of American culture, having been raised on Coca-Cola, Kellogg's

Lennon arrives in New York to be espoused by leaders of the radical left

corn flakes and Elvis Presley (a statement that filled with great sadness those of us who had been buoyed by the Beatles precisely because they had freed us from a cultural inferiority complex).

Yoko, having spent much of her life in New York, was in any case keen to move back there, where she could feel more herself and less an appendage of John. Once he arrived, John was certainly seduced by the atmosphere, which was hardly surprising. England had always seemed stuffy, unimaginative and resistant to change. He found the opposite circumstances in New York, and these suited him perfectly. Throughout the century, America had seemed the land of opportunity to millions of immigrants, and that was how it now appeared to John; because America (or at any rate, New York) had an open mind about Art, and was prepared to take seriously the unusual, the challenging, the bizarre and the just plain stupid. If John said that he was a serious artist, then he could at least be certain that New York would hear him out. In Britain, he was considered a popular songwriter-musician of extraordinary talent, no more and no less; his extra-curricular activities were scorned.

In any case, John was given no opportunity to weigh the alternative choices of New York or England's Home Counties. He'd hardly set foot in America than he was welcomed by Jerry Rubin and Abbie Hoffman, leaders of the Yippie movement, and the people best qualified to instruct Lennon in the politics of the American New Left.

This was perfect. Lennon was already at the centre of the radical left/avant-garde circle whose acceptance he so much craved. There had been no such community in England (though Lennon had been pleased to give an interview to Tariq Ali's *Red Mole*), and the fact that the New York counter-culture

espoused him so readily made it certain that he would stay.

Of course, it was inevitable anyway that Lennon would get hooked on New York: there are far more television stations there than in Britain.

Before Lennon left England, though, he had completed work on a new album, *Imagine*, and had also shot thousands of feet of film to accompany it.

The album was released on the Apple label in September 1971, and was a commercial success, becoming Lennon's best-selling solo album prior to *Double Fantasy*. However, the signs were unmistakable: Lennon was in a confused mental state, and had lost the sureness of touch, that perfect musical instinct that had served him while the Beatles were still *ensemble*; *Imagine* was the beginning of his long day's journey into night.

In its way, *John Lennon/Plastic Ono Band* had been a perfect album and, although no one could possibly have asked that its sequel should display an equivalent emotional intensity, one had expected that the metaphysical journey of discovery that he had undertaken on the earlier album would have led him somewhere. Instead, *Imagine* made all those harrowing experiences seem irrelevant, since Lennon still seemed uncertain and directionless – sporting his emotional scars one minute, and turning aggressive and vituperative the next. *Imagine* was the album with which Lennon's barely-begun solo career fell apart. All that old artistic self-confidence – cockiness, really – had been dissipated.

Perhaps *Imagine's* most readily apparent quality was the earnestness of the attacks on Paul McCartney. 'How Do You Sleep?' was the track which attracted most attention, since it was a brazen, vitriolic broadside on McCartney, in whose *Ram* album, as we have noted, Lennon had detected hostile references to himself. A track called '3 Legs' contained the lines, "*When I thought you was my friend/But you let me down/Put my heart around the bend*", which seemed to give Lennon the idea that the album contained unpleasant veiled messages to him, and he interpreted everything else in this light.

Such behaviour speaks volumes for Lennon's egocentricity (and, one supposes, his paranoia). Anyway, Lennon plotted revenge, and he did so in a way which left no room for ambiguity: "*The only thing you've done was yesterday/And since you've gone you're just another day.*" The track had opened with the sounds of an orchestra tuning up (echoing those used at the start of *Sergeant Pepper's Lonely Hearts Club Band*), and so the song took aim at the history of the Beatles, as well as at Paul individually. Most unforgivably, Lennon wrote, "*Those freaks was right when they said you was dead.*" It was a wholly malevolent character assassination. As usual, when Lennon got the urge to do something, he did it with unrestrained gusto. 'How Do You Sleep?' wasn't even the only nasty song. There was also a truly vicious track called 'Crippled Inside', which no doubt referred to Paul in particular and a large part of the human race in general. The arrangement of the song was bizarre, for it was sung at a jaunty pace over a bouncy rhythm that quite belied the offensiveness of the lyrics. (The type of accompaniment, in fact, was used much more appositely on 'Oh, Yoko', one of the album's best songs.)

The final part of this three-pronged attack on his erstwhile partner was a postcard tucked inside the album, of Lennon grasping a pig by the ears - a photograph that crudely and pointlessly lampooned the cover of *Ram*; what made the whole thing so sad was that the *Ram* art-work was so puerile that there

was little point in parodying it.

Of the other tracks on *Imagine*, there was one, 'How?', that might easily have cropped up on the previous album, and another, 'It's So Hard' that had more than a hint of self-pity. There were a couple of semi-political pieces, 'I Don't Want To Be A Soldier', which was fairly disposable, and 'Gimme Some Truth', which was excellent. This was a left-over from the Beatle days, from the 'Get Back' sessions in fact, and it showed Lennon's cutting wit and expert free-association for once used to good effect.

After the starkness of *John Lennon/Plastic Ono Band*, *Imagine* was a commercial album, in the most conventional terms. There were five tracks a side, extensive use of synthesised strings, and no funny bits, spoken interjections, contributions from Yoko, or 'Revolution No. 9's. This was mainstream pop music, a far cry from what Lennon had been delivering in recent years.

This change of direction is thought to have been prompted by Allen Klein, although the use of Phil Spector as co-producer was also felt to have been significant. In fact, Spector clearly thought that he had been employed strictly in the role of assistant producer (virtually in the same capacity as he had filled on *Plastic Ono Band*), since John was in charge throughout. The commercial bias of *Imagine*, then, was clearly of Lennon's own doing. Although he never admitted it, he probably agreed with Klein, and was worried about falling sales.

For all these reasons, therefore, *Imagine* seemed confused. In fact, when it was first released, it seemed such a crushing disappointment that it took me literally years to appreciate that its title-track is one of the pinnacles of achievement in rock music.

'Imagine' condenses Lennon's political philosophy - the unattainable utopia - better

The authorities revoked Lennon's visa extension, initiating a near-ceaseless 4-year struggle

than anything else he ever wrote; its simple humanitarianism is perfectly communicated. The song is a classic. When released as a single in the U.S., it went into the Top 10. It's noticeable, though, that Lennon's move across the Atlantic meant that he quickly lost touch with events in Britain, because EMI didn't release 'Imagine' as a single in the U.K. until 1975, at which time Lennon was baffled to discover that it had not been issued as a single in the first place.

'Imagine', 'Gimme Some Truth' and 'Oh, Yoko'; the other outstanding track on the album was 'Jealous Guy', another song that was distinguished by its emotional honesty. As a song of apology to Yoko, it was very moving – and probably very necessary; there is little doubt that for all the apparently blissful contentment of the John–Yoko relationship, there were private occasions when John could treat Yoko spitefully.

For all *Imagine*'s flaws, therefore, it was a work of considerable merit, and it was not until he recorded *Double Fantasy*, nine years later, that John made a superior album. For the moment, *Imagine* marked the conclusion of his work in Britain. Even by the time of its release, he had already saturated himself in the sights and sounds of New York, where, from his point of view, everything was going spectacularly well spectacularly quickly.

For a fortnight from October 9, Yoko had an exhibition at the Everson Museum of Art in Syracuse, New York; the show was entitled This Is Not Here – also the message on a sign that had adorned the threshold of their Tittenhurst Park home.

Lennon was billed as guest artist, and he was delighted with the whole arrangement, for it meant that his wife was at last being treated as a serious artist. Whether or not the exhibition consisted of serious art was open to question. It included Yoko's usual selec-

tion of flotsam and jetsam of the consumer society, highlighted in a new way. Ray Connolly notes that one of the exhibits was a block of ice in the shape of a 'T', which was slowly melting, and which was captioned "Iced Tea". John exuberantly predicted that in the next few months, Yoko would be placed by critics in the vanguard of a new Art movement.

In the months leading up to Christmas, John identified himself with a number of left-wing causes. During the period of the exhibition they staged a protest in support of civil rights for American Indians. Later they performed benefit concerts at the Apollo theatre in New York, after the Attica state prison shootings, and then in Ann Arbor, Michigan, in support of John Sinclair, a leading counter-culture figure who'd just been handed an absurdly severe prison sentence for possession of a small amount of cannabis.

These activities, disparate though they may have been, did not go unheeded by the U.S. authorities, who managed to discern an overall pattern to them. Lennon, they felt, had become the instrument of the New Left. They were anxious lest he should be used to mobilise funds, rally adolescent opinion, and oppose the incumbent president, Richard Nixon, during his campaign for re-election. What particularly worried them was that a mood of insurgency could develop, and climax in a massive popular demonstration at the August 1972 Republican convention in San Diego, similar to the one which had occurred at the Chicago Democratic Convention four years earlier.

As events were subsequently to show, the Nixon administration was characterised from top to bottom by an obsessive paranoia. Such an atmosphere resulted not merely in Watergate, but also the whole catalogue of dirty tricks which preceded it and which, in a sense, did ensure the re-election of the president. Lennon was perhaps fortunate to be the target of less offensive practices than other left-wingers, although he certainly didn't escape harassment. On the contrary, his phone was tapped, his room bugged, and he was constantly followed; although when he mentioned this latter fact on a national television programme, the shadowing stopped – proof, certainly, that his enemies knew that they were behaving illegally.

However, it was not difficult for the authorities to apply more legitimate pressure on Lennon. Early in 1972 a Senate Internal Security sub-committee of the Judiciary Committee sent a memo to Senator Strom Thurmond, outlining the reasons why Lennon was a significant feather in the left's cap, how disruptive an influence he could prove, simply by dint of his pre-eminence, and why he should be deported. Thurmond passed the memo to John Mitchell, director of the campaign to re-elect the president, who was shortly to become a leading celebrity in the Watergate affair. Mitchell passed it on to deputy attorney-general, Richard Kleindienst, who concurred with the sentiments, and asked, "Do we have any basis to deny his admittance?" Yes, they did – Lennon's 1968 conviction in London for possession of cannabis. Lennon had always maintained his innocence of this particular charge, arguing that the drug had been planted, and that he'd only pleaded guilty to spare Yoko nervous stress during a difficult time of pregnancy. When the policeman involved was later found guilty of just the offence Lennon alleged (planting evidence on a suspect), his story seemed to be confirmed.

However miniscule this evidence of a criminal nature, the U.S. authorities doggedly pursued the point, and on March 6

1972 the visa extension which had only lately been granted to him was revoked. Initially, it seemed as though Lennon would have to leave. On April 29 even a plea from the Mayor of New York, John Lindsay, to allow Lennon to remain was brushed aside. But Lennon himself stuck to his task as pertinaciously as the authorities stuck to theirs, and the business dragged on and on. It was to occupy him almost ceaselessly for the next four years, causing him considerable stress and heartache. He appeared in court on a number of occasions, and altogether was reckoned to spend over half a million dollars in fighting his case. He tried every ploy he could think of, and on one occasion asked the Queen for a royal pardon, so that his drug conviction would be expunged from the record, and he'd be allowed to reside in the U.S.; perhaps if he hadn't returned his M.B.E. so peremptorily, she would have consented.

One can therefore add to the list of reasons why Lennon so adamantly wanted to sojourn in America the very fact that they were attempting to deport him; the more determined they became in their efforts to be rid of him, the more determined he became to stay.

To return to the beginning of the struggle: the initial difficulty over the visa renewal in March 1972 occurred at an unfortunate time for Lennon. First of all, the business which he and Yoko had originally gone to New York to attend to – i.e. the custody of Yoko's daughter, Kyoko – was still not settled; and furthermore, John had lately been planning to go on the road again, with Elephant's Memory.

During his early days in New York, John recorded very little. However he did go into the studio at the end of October to record a Christmas single, with Phil Spector as co-

producer, and a Plastic Ono Band that on this occasion consisted of Nicky Hopkins (keyboards), Hugh McCracken (guitar) and Jim Keltner (drums), and also the Harlem Community Choir. The song also featured the Christmas greeting that John and Yoko had become accustomed to delivering every year, usually by way of giant advertising hoardings in the world's capital cities: War Is Over (If You Want It). Thus, the message that John is delivering is his and Yoko's, and it fits naturally into the context of the song. He could handle such material with ease; it was the second-hand propaganda that he tended to use badly. But 'Happy Xmas (War Is Over)' is one of Lennon's best songs.

Unfortunately, it was mishandled from a marketing point of view. It was released too late to make much impact on the Christmas market in the U.S. (where, in any case, Christmas singles were very much a rarity. Lennon was probably not aware of this, since they appear with annual regularity in the U.K.). By this time, much of the Beatle product tended to be released in the U.S. before it appeared in the U.K., and so the U.K. release of 'Happy Xmas' had to be delayed until the following year.

Since that had represented Lennon's only

recording activity, he was obviously keen to return to business. Thus, he had been looking for a New York-based rock band to work with, and he fixed on Elephant's Memory after Jerry Rubin played him a tape of theirs. Probably the group represented just what John was looking for; they had a gutsy, ballsy sound, although they seemed to lack invention, imagination and direction of their own, and were not especially distinguished. They had contributed a couple of excellent tracks to the soundtrack of John Schlesinger's film *Midnight Cowboy*, but that had been a couple of years earlier. The group line-up had been changed in the interim, although leader Stan Bronstein was still present.

Lennon adopted them for a time virtually as his backing band, and made his next album with them. This was, unfortunately, a disaster.

Some Time In New York City was an attempt by Lennon to document the *causes célèbres* of the time. These included those he had already espoused (the shooting of inmates in Attica prison, John Sinclair), and areas of fresh concern for him: Northern Ireland, the imprisoned radical Angela Davis, and one song about feminism, 'Woman Is The Nigger Of The World'. In most cases, the songs were awful and the lyrics trite. There was no political analysis (good heavens, no), just a banal and strident regurgitation of the issues of radical concern. As had been the case with 'Power To The People', it was John once again spitting out slogans.

The album was designed as a newspaper – with columns, photographs and headlines – and John later explained that the problem had been that he'd been trying to be a journalist, reporting on contemporary events, and that his mistake was to write about events as they were being described to him, rather than as he saw them himself. He'd stopped adhering to his own personal vision, the very thing that had always made him so unique an artist, and had leased out his art to the New Left activists. The results were predictably terrible, but this was a tragedy not just for John's art, but for his spiritual well-being. To quote Roy Carr and Tony Tyler from *The Beatles: An Illustrated Record*: "Lennon was living in a New York radical-chic ghetto, surrounded by committed politial figures and a fair percentage of the usual big-city cultural vampires. Having deliberately rejected world leadership *as a Beatle*, Lennon allowed himself to be manipulated *as John Lennon*, ex-Beatle."

Certainly, little of Lennon's idiosyncratic humour penetrated this album. The cover did arouse some fuss in the U.S., since some retailers refused to handle it unless the mocked-up photograph of Richard Nixon and Chairman Mao dancing naked together was obscured.

Some Time In New York City also boasted a free album (though inevitably the 'freeness' of the extra album caused an inordinately high price to be placed on the main one), which featured music from two John and Yoko live performances. The first was a concert with Frank Zappa and the Mothers of Invention on June 6 1971 at the Fillmore East, New York; and the second was an age-old UNICEF benefit they had played at the Lyceum ballroom in London in 1969 with George Harrison and sundry members of the Delaney and Bonnie entourage.

The album enjoyed some commercial U.S. success, but very little in the U.K. For someone who could reasonably claim to be the world's foremost rock artiste, this was tantamount to complete failure. It must have been shattering. Lennon's whole approach was called into question, and it is no wonder that he retreated from it almost immediately.

Not that he abandoned Elephant's Memory.

He seems to have believed that they were nevertheless capable of creating good rock music together, and on August 30 1972 he headlined with them (and Yoko, of course) at a charity concert in Madison Square Garden. The two shows were in aid of retarded children, and the net proceeds from the gig ($1.5 million, amassed from the gate receipts and the sale of the television rights) were donated to three New York charities, so that small residences could be built at Willowbrook children's homes where the children could receive individual attention. The project was thus known as One To One, and on the day of the concert Mayor Lindsay declared that it was a 'One To One' Day in New York.

The whole affair was thus a complete success. Apart from anything else, Lennon himself was, by all reports, in excellent form, and gave a superb performance; that he has always been a truly great vocalist has never seriously been questioned, and apparently this concert offered yet further confirmation of that. The occasion seems to have been a splendid one, and no doubt did much to expunge the memory of the wretched *Some Time In New York City*.

In Britain, of course, virtually nothing was reported in the press of the concert, and no television company had the gumption to pick up the rights to the show. The British media still unanimously portrayed Lennon as the Beatle who had lost his marbles, and they weren't about to do anything to prejudice their prejudice, as it were. Consequently, this act of redemption went unappreciated by the British public, and thus Lennon really paid the price for *Some Time*. In many respects, his career in the U.K. never recovered from it until he died.

Meanwhile, John and Yoko worked with Elephant's Memory on one other occasion.

'Mind Games' – caught between being a manic political lunatic and a musician again . . .

In return for the help which the group had given, John and Yoko produced their album. *Elephant's Memory* appeared on the Apple label in September 1972. It was not successful, and there was no further collaboration.

Lennon subsequently began to shed his radical associates, as though that was another phase of his life that had become passé; though this time his characteristic boredom was probably laced with sheer panic, once it had become apparent that their company was having a malign effect on his artistry.

Meanwhile his time was more and more occupied simply with his struggle to remain in the U.S. In March 1973 he was again ordered to leave, and again appealed against the decision. There was, though, some good news for him and Yoko that month, when the latter was finally granted custody of Kyoko (now eight years old). Ironically they never saw her after that, since Tony Cox once more took flight with her, and John's little local difficulty meant that it was impossible for them to set off in pursuit.

John had been so preoccupied with domestic affairs that it was summer when he suddenly realised that it was time for him to work on another album.

A year had elapsed since the release of *Some Time*, and during 1973 the only time he had gone to the studios had been to help Ringo, recording 'I'm The Greatest', a song he'd written for Ringo's new album. Now, he entered the Record Plant, New York on his own behalf – as usual, with little material prepared in advance.

For once, he was unable to rise to the occasion – clearly he was disorientated and uncertain of his muse after the *Some Time* catastrophe. The best one can say of the album is that it's exceptionally well produced. (There was no Spector in attendance this time. No matter; production seemed to be merely another facet of the art of making records that Lennon had mastered.)

Although the album's title-track, 'Mind Games', was excellent, there was only one other that rose to the same standard, 'Bring On The Lucie (Freda Peeple)', and the lyrics of each showed Lennon speedily backtracking from his political rhetoric of the previous year. "*We don't care what flag you're waving,*" he sings, showing the door to the political ideologies he'd embraced so ardently the previous year.

What political sentiment there is on the album is more idiosyncratic. John and Yoko offer one and all citizenship of a conceptual country, Nutopia, which, in line with the ideals adumbrated on 'Imagine', has, "No land, no boundaries, no passports, only people." After the glib didacticism of the pro-Irish songs on *Some Time*, Lennon was now cleverly undermining the patriot game. The last track on the album was devoted to the Nutopian International Anthem. It was silent.

Mostly, however, *Mind Games* consisted of so-so songs that hardly lodged in the memory. It was not a bad album, but it was neither exciting nor encouraging; one had not expected an album's worth of filler material from John Lennon. He explained its somewhat tepid appeal by describing it as "An interim record, between being a manic political lunatic and being a musician again."

Naturally, the album also contained its customary quota of songs dedicated to Yoko. 'Aisumasen (I'm Sorry)' featured some early attempts at Japanese; 'One Day (At A Time)', 'Out The Blue' and 'I Know (I Know)' are all tender love songs, while 'You Are Here' sees their relationship in terms of East meets West ("From Liverpool to Tokyo", etc.).

However, before the record had even been

released, he had parted company from Yoko – virtually their first separation since they had spent that fateful weekend together in Weybridge in May 1968.

Clearly, John had been under considerable pressure, much of which was caused by his running battle with the immigration authorities over his status in the U.S. No doubt he was becoming disillusioned with New York as well. He had been at the centre of the city's counter-culture, but had not found true happiness – only, perhaps, the rather unpleasant feeling that he was being used. "Did I do all that," he said later, "just so that Jerry Rubin could get a decent job?" Thus he had moved out of that circle, but had found nothing to replace it. Thirdly, there must have been some artistic dissatisfaction. For the first time ever, he had just recorded an album with which he was not entirely happy.

So, he did what he always did when his life seemed to have reached a cul-de-sac. He fired the ejector seat. As Lennon himself told it, "One day I went out for a cup of coffee and some papers, and I didn't come back." He didn't have a vast range of contacts in the U.S. – very few, in fact. So he flew to Los Angeles to look up Phil Spector. He'd been thinking of doing a rock'n'roll album; a 100% rock'n'roll album.

While John had been wrecking the foundations of his own career, and then attempting to piece it back together, Paul had been involuntarily pursuing a similar course of action back in London.

During this early stage of their solo careers, Lennon and McCartney affected each other intensely. It was generally Lennon who acted, and McCartney who reacted. The latter, for example, was particularly hurt by Lennon's lengthy, soul-bearing *Rolling Stone* interview in which he dismantled the Beatles' legend piece by piece, and fired a few broadsides at

his old partner along the way.

There was one revealing quote. John averred that Paul would probably admire his new album (*John Lennon/Plastic Ono Band*): "I think it'll probably scare him into doing something decent. And then he'll scare me into doing something decent and I'll scare him. . . ." It was a pattern which Lennon later diagnosed as a 'sibling rivalry'.

This rivalry undoubtedly existed, and it is clear that each was constantly keeping a weather-eye on the activities of the other, even though the full extent of the Atlantic separated them. (In fact, once McCartney had been found guilty of possession of drugs in Sweden in 1972, contact between them was suddenly rendered impossible, since McCartney could not at that time enter the U.S. because of the conviction, and Lennon could not leave it, ironically for the very same reason.) However, far from scaring each other into reputable work, they seemed to have only a deleterious effect on each other.

After the *Rolling Stone* interview, McCartney said little, but it was clear that his confidence was shaken and that, for all the years of Beatle predominance, he had no clear idea of which path to take as a solo artiste – and neither, of course, did Lennon. McCartney, though, at least was determined to resume live performances. Again, the way he wanted to do it – slowly and systematically – was in contra-distinction to John, whose own appearances were occasional, arbitrary and invariably well-publicised.

Paul wanted to take his own group touring, since he'd long felt that what the Beatles had lacked in their latter stages had been direct contact with their audience. That much is evident from *Let It Be*. He had even suggested then to the others what he was proposing now to himself: that they should take to the road, and play small club dates –

Paul, in search of an audience, forms Wings

unheralded, unadvertised, un-hyped; but John had scoffed and the idea had been dropped.

Paul now wanted to revive it on his own behalf, and to this end formed his own band, Wings. Like John, he reserved a place for his wife – and Linda had a more considerable function than Yoko usually served, for she was given responsibility for keyboards, which Paul had been teaching her throughout the year. An old friend, Denny Laine, who had first attracted Paul's attention as the vocalist on the Moody Blues' 'Go Now', came in on guitar, and the line-up was completed by Denny Seiwell, whose drumming had already featured prominently on *Ram*.

No sooner had the group been assembled than McCartney put it to the test in the studio, recording *Wild Life* at the end of the summer.

Wild Life was an album of quite extraordinary banality. After *Ram* had backfired, McCartney moved too quickly in trying to repair the damage. Further, he had decided that albums needed to be created instantaneously, in order to promote urgency, vitality, earthiness – the kind of qualities that rock 'n' roll was theoretically supposed to exemplify. It was a recording technique that had supposedly always worked for Bob Dylan.

However, the point McCartney had overlooked was that his particular attributes were of a quite different kind. His songs benefited from being carefully and painstakingly developed in the studio. In many ways it is incredible that, after fifteen years in the business, he was approaching a work in the most inappropriate way of all. In itself, that is evidence enough of the individual disarray and aesthetic dislocation of the Beatles once they had finally realised they had to make their own way in the world.

Wild Life was bereft of redeeming features. The only track that was not a hopeless embarrassment was a version of the old Peaches and Herb song, 'Love Is Strange'. It is almost the only time the post-Beatle McCartney has ever covered outside material (Paul Simon's 'Richard Cory' was included on *Wings Over America*), and that it should be the only memorable track on the album shows just how far the powers of creativity of the most successful living songwriter had temporarily ebbed.

The album was a disaster in every possible respect. The front cover was simply a photograph of the newly-decorated Wings, bare of either credits or album title. Now, the Beatles could get away with a plain photograph (and did, on *Abbey Road*), and McCartney, like Lennon, might have managed it on his own; but how could he expect to pull it off when he was striving for anonymity in the midst of his new group?

It was absurd. Paul was on the one hand trying to portray himself merely as one of the boys in the band, and thereby disavowing any special claims to pre-eminence, and on the other assuming that the album would sell purely on the strength of those very special claims, since he'd deliberately deprived it of other marketable features.

(Probably, the cover photograph was yet another example of sibling rivalry – or sibling imitation. In 1970, Lennon had used a full-sleeve shot of himself and Yoko in idyllic, sun-speckled rural surroundings for the front of *John Lennon/Plastic Ono Band*; in 1971 Paul used a full-sleeve shot of himself and Linda (and Wings) in idyllic, sun-speckled ditto for the front of *Wild Life*. It always seemed more than a coincidence,

especially since there is a certain record business machismo attached to being able to sell your album without putting your name on the front; and the covers are very similar, especially in colouration.)

If the *Wild Life* front cover was a mistake, the back was even worse. This provided an awful drawing and inappropriate lettering, the combined effect of which was to make the album seem like a 12/6d. bargain-bin offer, and sleeve-notes, written by a certain 'Clint Harrigan', of quite unbelievable gaucheness. The notes explained the genesis of Wings and the album. "In this wrapper is the music they made," gushed Mr Harrigan, as though the fact had taken him by surprise. "Can you dig it?" he concluded, using an unpardonable expression that is somehow meant to insinuate that the onus is on the listener to enjoy the music, rather than on the music to be worthy of enjoyment.

Perhaps Clint was just a pseudonym for Paul, who was ensuring that the outside of the package was of a tackiness commensurate with what was inside it. Whatever the reason, it should be remembered that the smug and crude practice of filling the back cover of an album with sycophantic sleeve-notes was one that had originally been killed off by the Beatles. In resurrecting it, McCartney was not simply debasing his own solo career, but also nullifying another of the Beatles' achievements. (This might seem a negligible point. By no means. The golden years of the Beatles were distinguished by a rejection both of business cant and of sleazy marketing ploys. The Beatles always knew how to sell their music, but they made sure that it sold on the quality of the music itself. McCartney now seemed to be turning back the clock.)

Shortly afterwards, Wings were brought up to a five-piece by the addition of Henry McCullough (guitar), formerly of the Grease

Paul had been deliberately striking attitudes, and being self-consciously calculating. It didn't work.

Band. This new line-up made 'Give Ireland Back To The Irish', a song recorded and released in February 1972 in the wake of the 'Bloody Sunday' Londonderry shootings.

This remains the only controversial political gesture of McCartney's entire career. It was hard to resist the feeling at the time, and is harder still in retrospect, that he was desperately hoping to repair his shattered credibility by this one solitary gesture; at a stroke he would show that John wasn't the only concerned, politically aware ex-Beatle, and also that he, Paul, wasn't the marshmallow man everybody suddenly seemed to think.

Like Lennon's least successful musical diatribes, 'Give Ireland' is a self-conscious, awkward song quite lacking in melodicism or charm. Although Lennon was shortly to rise to the bait on and show on *Some Time In New York City* that he could do far worse than this, 'Give Ireland', which was banned by all radio and television stations and became a minor hit, gave the appearance of being an exploitation single every bit as much as 'tribute' singles that are rushed out in the wake of the death of a star name. (In defence of both Lennon and McCartney, however, it should be remembered that they came from Liverpool, a city which enjoyed regular contact with Ireland, and that therefore they would have been well grounded in Irish nationalist rhetoric and sentiment.)

McCartney's next single was more bizarre still. 'Mary Had A Little Lamb' was perhaps an attempt to make those who had censored the previous effort look foolish, by implying that twee songs of nursery rhyme simplicity were perhaps all the media could stomach. Alternatively, he may just have been reassuring those members of his presumed audience who were under eight and over eighty (a constituency he diligently canvassed).

Whatever the reason, it was equally embarrassing, albeit for very different reasons. No, the same reason: in both cases, Paul had been deliberately striking attitudes, and being self-consciously calculating. It didn't work. Like Ringo, he was no good at playing roles; he could only act naturally.

Before the release of 'Mary Had A Little Lamb' however, he finally had a chance to do just that when the tour that had been at the back of his mind for so long finally got underway. On February 8, 1972, he turned up at a Nottingham college asking if his band could perform there the following day. His wish that the concert be kept a close secret was respected, and Wings duly made their debut the following day, entirely free from the intimidating attention of the press.

It was a sensible ploy, given how difficult it was for any of the ex-Beatles to return to live performance. After all, both Harrison and Lennon had already appeared at major New York venues, and starting at the top was something McCartney absolutely wanted to avoid – both so that the group could have time to develop naturally, and also so that some kind of audience contact could be resumed. Members of theatre companies are frequently lamenting the lack of rapport in the West End and preaching the virtues of playing small halls throughout the provinces – so why should it be any different for rock stars? And so, being who he was, Paul did it the only way he could, clandestinely. (Indeed, that was also the way in which Harrison had resumed live performances, three years after the Beatles had stopped touring, by making unannounced, and unobtrusive, appearances with Delaney and Bonnie.)

Thus, Wings toured the country by van, playing what were effectively a series of low-key warm-up gigs, and featuring a repertoire which featured definitely no Beatles material.

Paul and Linda, relaxing on the open roof of their double decker bus, at the start of their tour in the South of France.

McCartney quickly felt confident enough in his band to undertake more conventional shows, although he chose halls in continental cities, once again making sure that the full glare of the media did not fall on the group.

In fact, he didn't manage to avoid the front pages even then, but that was less to do with the nature of his tour than with the fact that he was arrested on drugs charges in Gothenburg, Sweden, in August. The incident did not prove to be an isolated one, for the following month it happened again. This time he was at home on his Scottish farm when local police accused him of cultivating cannabis in his greenhouse. "A fan sent me some seeds, and I planted them to see what they were," he told the court. A likely story; but the fine of £100 seemed lenient for a man in his position and, after all, his credibility was beginning to soar.

Towards the end of the year, he released another single – the third of the year, the second to be banned. This was 'Hi, Hi, Hi', which the powers-that-be construed as a pro-drugs song. A misconception, certainly, but in view of McCartney's recent behaviour, perhaps one could hardly blame them for that, even if one could not condone their readiness to act so censoriously.

In fact, 'Hi, Hi, Hi' was McCartney's best single to date, a raunchy rocker, which was complemented by a superb B-side, 'C Moon', which demonstrated McCartney's musical versatility in that he perfectly harnessed reggae rhythms to his own requirements. Its sales suffered some slight disruption because of the Christmas holiday period, but even so it reached No. 5 in the U.K. charts.

The tide began to turn with the combined critical and commercial success of this single; clearly, McCartney was putting it all together again. Sensing that his hour had almost arrived, he worked indefatigably throughout 1973.

However, he continued to exasperate his audience a while longer, and *Red Rose Speedway*, released in May, gave little hint that a full-scale resurrection was in the offing; but however inoffensive and undemanding the album seemed at the time of its release, in retrospect it can be seen as a vital link in the chain. It is finely crafted, and avoids both the self-indulgences and the self-conscious sparseness of production of earlier solo efforts. 'One More Kiss' showed that he was back in the business of composing charming songs that could be sentimental without being cloying, and unpretentious without being banal. Once again McCartney was concentrating on his strong points, and bearing in mind the demands of the market-place. In deference to the latter, he even allowed the album to be credited to 'Paul McCartney and Wings', and made sure that his mug was slapped unmistakably on the front cover.

Commercial nous was rewarded with commercial success. In the U.S. the album took over the No. 1 spot from the Beatle retrospective albums (*1962–66*; *1967–70*) that Allen Klein had lately compiled to replenish the dwindling stockpiles. Sales were assisted by two factors. First of all, the fact that the album produced a huge hit single, 'My Love', a melodramatic ballad in the same vein as 'The Long And Winding Road' (though, unlike that, not over-produced). Secondly, McCartney had just debuted on U.S. television, starring in his own hour-long entertainment show, *James Paul McCartney*.

James Paul McCartney found the lad himself trying on a new hat – that of all-round entertainer, as conceived in terms of commercial television – and it didn't fit. Not surprisingly, since prime-time TV has never been kind to rock performers. The two forms of entertainment are almost certainly incompatible – rock is all rough edges, where commercial TV fare has been planed to a smooth finish. "Even those of us who were rooting for Paul," writes Nicholas Schaffner in *The Beatles Forever*, "found it hard to suppress our groans as Wings nuzzled sheep to the strains of 'Mary Had A Little Lamb', and as Paul tried to make passionate faces while crooning 'My Love', looking instead as if he'd just sucked a lemon."

This was made for Lord Grade's network, and thus marked an end to the hostilities between him and Paul, which had erupted when Grade's ATV had won control of Northern Songs, the Lennon–McCartney publishing company. Paul's response had been to co-credit compositions henceforth to

himself and Linda, so that at least half the incoming royalties were outside Grade's control. Once McCartney had agreed to do the television special, Grade agreed to stop contesting this manoeuvre.

Another commission McCartney had undertaken was to write the theme music for the new James Bond movie, *Live And Let Die*. The music appeared together with the film, in the summer of that year, and, although the words were suspect, the song itself was good, and was excellently scored by George Martin. His work with Paul on the soundtrack of the film represented the only time that he had worked with any of the ex-Beatles during the entire decade. It was, though, a highly successful collaboration. (McCartney was to get even more low-brow the following year, when he agreed to devise a new arrangement for the theme of *Crossroads*, the most banal, most regularly castigated, of all British TV soap operas, and something else that came to the millions courtesy of Lord Grade. The music he devised for the programme can still be heard on Paul's *Venus And Mars* album, though not on *Crossroads* itself, which quickly reverted to the original music.)

It was against this background of mounting commercial success that Wings finally set out on their first bona fide U.K. tour in the summer of 1973.

The group passed their audition. All the concerts were well-received. By now, there was a plentiful supply of Wings' own material. McCartney must have been particularly gratified when 13-year-olds, asked to name their favourite McCartney composition, frequently opted for 'My Love' or 'Hi, Hi, Hi'. He felt that it was now possible to start including the occasional Beatle song in the show.

During this period it was John and Paul

who made all the running, publicly squabbling and releasing albums that were unworthy of them. George and Ringo let them get on with it, and each retreated from the glare of publicity. George took a well-earned (though, as we shall see, inadvisable) rest after the exertions of putting together two triple albums in just over a year, and basked comfortably in his new-found public esteem after the huge success of the Bangla Desh project; in June 1972 both Harrison and Ravi Shankar were presented with special UNICEF awards by Kurt Waldheim, U.N. Secretary--General.

Ringo released 'Back Off Boogaloo', a single which Harrison had produced for him, in April 1972. It therefore appeared almost exactly a year after its predecessor, 'It Don't Come Easy', and proved to be every bit as ebullient. The song was, perhaps, slightly inferior, but that would have been quibbling. It gave Ringo another respectable hit single and confirmed that he and Harrison, dark horses both, were the ones who had managed their solo careers more purposefully and intelligently.

Not that Ringo was too preoccupied with his career as a recording star. He was in the throes of becoming a film director, temporarily at least.

His filming activities during 1971 had had disappointing results. Neither *200 Motels* nor *Blindman* had been judged successful, either by critics or audiences. So, having long been fascinated by photography, he decided to direct a film himself, which he financed through Apple (which, all those years, had had a dormant film division).

The film he made was *Born To Boogie*, a documentary built around Marc Bolan's T. Rex, and their appearances at the Empire Pool, Wembley in March 1972. There were those who were prepared to argue that '70s-style T. Rexstasy was the contemporary substitute for '60s Beatlemania, and hence it seemed an appropriate topic for Ringo. In the event, T. Rex didn't last the course, though Bolan, who was killed in a car

Ringo finds himself in 'That'll Be The Day'

accident in September 1977, is fondly remembered by a legion of fans.

Ringo's film was not hugely popular, though he did manage to convey the excitement of the moment. However, the experience was probably a salutary one for him. By studying in such close detail the pop heroes of the moment he was perhaps able to put the Beatles in better perspective than Lennon, McCartney or Harrison could.

The next year Ringo made his only completely successful solo film appearance, starring with David Essex in *That'll Be The Day*. The role was perfect, since it allowed Ringo to be a 1950's teddy boy; more or less the part in which he'd always seen himself. He performed with splendid aplomb, and struck up a perfect working partnership with David Essex. The film was the poorer once Ringo had been written out of the story.

That'll Be The Day did so well that there was a sequel, *Stardust*. Ringo passed this one by, on the grounds that it would be documenting the music scene of the '60s, and he thought that the fictional events of the movie might prove disconcertingly similar to the actual events of his life-story. Further, he didn't want to be part of anything in which there was a risk of denigrating the Beatles' legend. Unlike John and Paul, that was something he had no wish either to undermine or ignore. He'd always been a Beatles fan.

Having kept a low profile during 1972, George resumed business in June 1973 with *Living In The Material World*, an album which followed *1962–66*, *1967–70* and *Red Rose Speedway* to the top of the U.S. charts.

The first thing to say is that it was a very good album. George was firstly an excellent guitarist, and secondly an excellent producer, and, thirdly, a very talented songwriter – though no longer an under-rated one.

Most of the songs were affirmations of

It wasn't easy to put together a sequel to 'All Things Must Pass', but George was the one of the four who set himself up for a pratfall, because his timing was most awry.

George's faith, and earnest appeals to the listener to follow his spiritual code. Virtually the only song that belonged to the material world was 'Sue Me, Sue You Blues', a song about the increasing legal and financial complexities surrounding the Apple organisation. There was nothing wrong with the song itself; on the contrary, it featured some lovely slide guitar. It did, however, seem rather out of place. Clearly, the difficulties

inherent in striving for spiritual goals when you're a young and famous multi-millionaire are not to be underestimated, and George did show signs of grappling with the problem. For example, the album sleeve carried, amongst all the symbols of holiness, and 'All Glories To Sri Krishna' messages, a photograph of Harrison with his musicians (Nicky Hopkins, Klaus Voormann, Jim Keltner, Ringo – the usual lot) enjoying a hearty repast, passing the no-doubt vintage wine, while in the background the longest limousine in the world awaits their convenience.

George thus recognised the quandary, but lyrically never came to terms with it. His songs either preach the virtues of an ascetic, spiritual existence, or, like 'Sue Me . . .' (and, earlier, 'Taxman') are impatient with those who come between him and his money.

It was for reasons like this that the album was not warmly welcomed by many critics, most of whom found Harrison's lyrics solemn and sanctimonious. Certainly, the album did lack humour. "*Give me hope/Help me cope/With my heavy load*" wailed Harrison – surely he should have been joyous, being the fount of so much enlightenment?

Those who carped at the lyrics, or at Harrison himself, missed a great deal of the music, much of which was exceptionally fine. 'Don't Let Me Wait Too Long' and 'The Light That Lighted The World' could rank with his best compositions, while 'Give Me Love', the track released as a single, attracted heavy sales.

There were problems with one or two songs: 'Who Can See It' was ideal material for someone, though not Harrison who didn't have the vocal range to cope with it, and the title-song was a flop, mainly because Harrison sounded strange vainly trying to elide the syllables of 'material' so that it fitted the music.

Like Spector (from whom, of course, he had learned this part of his trade), Harrison went for a big, overall sound, with keyboards, acoustic guitars and accompanying strings all used prominently. There was one Spector co-production, the inclusion of which surprised many people, Spector included.

The song was 'Try Some, Buy Some', which George had written for Ronnie Spector,

Phil's ex-wife and former lead singer of the Ronettes, when she was attempting to re-launch her career in 1971. Spector had produced the song, giving it a treatment that was lavish and highly orchestrated even by his standards, but the song had not charted. Presumably Spector felt the same kind of disillusionment he had experienced when 'River Deep, Mountain High' by Ike and Tina Turner had been a flop in the U.S. Harrison, however, did not believe in discarding good ideas, and so he included the song here, having simply erased Ronnie's vocal track and substituted his own.

This was considered an underhand trick in some quarters. However, since the single had clearly not received the attention it merited, it could be argued that George was simply husbanding his resources carefully. Because the use of the song underlined an important point: Harrison was not a prolific songwriter.

Thus were his difficulties in putting together a sequel to *All Things Must Pass* compounded. First of all, he had a lot to live up to. He felt overwhelmed, not by the Beatles' legacy, but by his own extraordinary success with that album. Secondly, though, he was not able to release a successor promptly – or, indeed, for some considerable time. It took him two-and-a-half years to put together *Living In The Material World*.

In the event, the album simply arrived too late, and this was George's only significant mistake. The record business sometimes moves at a fast pace and by the time the album appeared the Beatles' elixir had been spirited away. In Britain, if not in the U.S.. a new pop music generation had arrived (as Ringo, after his filming stints with T. Rex, could have told him), which now wanted its own here-and-now heroes and was not prepared to swallow accepted truths about a somewhat mythic group called the Beatles, a group which had not given a British performance in the last eight years. By the time that *Living In The Material World* finally appeared, half the record-buying public thought that 'The Light That Lighted The World' referred to Gary Glitter.

Thus, audiences were less likely to be enamoured of the four ex-Beatles than they had been in 1970, and likewise critics were apt to be less respectful. George was the one of the four who set himself up for a pratfall, because his timing was most awry. After all, by the time that other acts had emerged to challenge the hegemony of the Beatles (or, if you like, to fill the vacuum created by their abdication), the other three had made some strides in re-assessing their own careers. John and Paul had already begun to recover from their worst blunders, and Ringo had begun to prove himself in new areas. George's lyrical themes and style of music were consistent with what he had been doing throughout his solo career. He was still immersed in Eastern mysticism, which to many now seemed simply another feature of an abandoned lifestyle. (All of which is not, of course, to decry George's spiritual convictions.)

The fact that *Living In The Material World* met with critical disapprobation and, in the U.K., disappointing sales, was unfortunate because the album was not intrinsically bad. Indeed, to reiterate the point, much of it was very good.

Naturally, the experience proved unsettling for George. His reaction was much the same as Paul's had been after *Ram*: panic and confusion, with resulting deteriorating artistic standards. In each case, both had been subject to some fierce critical contumely for which they were not prepared, and both reacted by producing albums that were vastly inferior to the ones originally lambasted.

This was hardly deliberate perversity on their parts. The fact is that they had always survived on instinct and mutual support. Suddenly, in a crisis, they realised that they had lost the latter and could no longer trust the former. They had been writing the rules themselves for so long that they were inevitably stymied in the short term when they had to accept that this was no longer their prerogative.

CHAPTER 6

Walls And Bridges

By the summer of 1973, the Beatle bubble had undoubtedly burst. There was no longer an aura of invincibility about them. True, they were still widely regarded as demi-gods – certainly among other members of their own profession, and also throughout the U.S. generally where their individual popularity was undimmed. In Britain, however, a new climate of opinion was developing, which meant that they could no longer count on an uncritical audience for their work (which is not to imply that they ever had). The press were also no longer inclined to talk of the four in reverential terms, and critics were very keen (as critics so often are) to knock down that which had been set up. The Beatles still occupied their pedestals, but from now on that was an exposed, rather than a comfortable, place to be. In their turn, Paul, John and George had all discovered this, while Ringo had yet to release a mainstream solo album. This was where the going got tough.

It may seem strange that people so successful as the four Beatles should have bothered at all about reviews, or taken any notice of what was said of them in the press. Surely such matters could no longer have been of

any importance? Reviews, of course, did influence sales, though only marginally.

Probably such concern may simply be a left-over of the days when the Beatles had enjoyed such cordial relationships with the entire press fraternity. It must have seemed bewildering when reviewers suddenly turned snide and became anxious to hurt.

On the whole, this attitude is simply a function of the competitiveness and obsessive fashionability of the rock press. But the Beatles themselves did contribute towards it in one sense. When they first became national celebrities, they took pleasure in being lionised, and, under Brian Epstein's careful guidance, made themselves regularly available to the press. Reporters were allowed to feel part of the Beatles' inner circle and, suitably flattered, gave them effusive write-ups.

Once Apple came into existence, they were even more beguiled. Now they could take pride in their proximity not simply to the Beatles themselves, but also to the Beatles' whisky, the Beatles' luncheon spreads, et cetera. Everyone who sampled the atmosphere ended up being seduced by it.

However the Apple junketings swiftly ceased once Allen Klein had arrived on the scene. It was inevitable that this would have happened anyway, and sooner rather than later. However, it wasn't only the last-days-of-Rome dissipation that was brought to an end. Klein's arrival also meant that the good relationships which the Beatles had consistently enjoyed with the press as a whole abruptly ended at the same time. Routine arrangements were countermanded; suddenly it made good sense to discourage journalists – partly because the Apple business became so sordid, and partly because Klein himself resented intrusion into his affairs.

The good press contacts which Brian Epstein had built up in the '60s had by now evaporated, and the Beatles enjoyed no relationships of any kind there during the '70s. This distancing was inevitably mistaken by members of the press as aloofness, and that it never was. For they all retained a fervent interest in contemporary music, and eagerly scoured the pages of the music press. When the bad reviews began to mount up in the '70s, therefore, they were hurt and disconcerted by them, and didn't appreciate that to a certain extent the reviews could be explained simply by the understandable (though not excusable) eagerness of critics to topple the high and mighty, a category into which the four certainly fitted. No doubt reviewers would have been more sympathetic had they met the Beatles, and had they realised that what they were writing still mattered greatly to them.

As the four Beatles withdrew ever more into their own private circle, surrounding themselves with their own retinue, so, from that time, did they lose the special relationship with the press that had prevailed from the beginning; and within a few years, press amity had been replaced by animosity.

However, it wasn't only the press from whom they withdrew. Whatever ties they'd had with EMI, their record company, were also sundered.

Apple was never a truly independent label, but merely a small unit within its parent organisation. However, Apple was run down during the early '70s, and by 1973, when all its basic functions of promoting and marketing records had been resumed by EMI, the Beatles had reached the point where they were in close contact with virtually no-one inside the company. In fact, it was an unwritten company rule: the Beatles were unapproachable.

This was mostly Klein's doing. Brian Epstein had always known that old-world courtesy and charm could move mountains, but Klein was not kindly disposed towards the social graces. He encouraged the Beatles to believe that they were stars who should avoid contact with common humanity (though, to be fair, this was a development that they'd have found hard to avoid, anyway; by the end of the decade, John Lennon had managed to resist it, with tragic results). More importantly, however, Klein also counselled them to employ more aggressive tactics in dealing with EMI, telling them (not without some justification) that the company had been virtually swindling them from the beginning. This they were only too willing to believe.

The result was that the Beatles remained aloof from the company, even though they were still signed to it and, as a matter of fact, were now receiving highly favourable royalties. This attitude should be contrasted with that of, say, Mick Jagger. When the Rolling Stones signed to EMI he went round the offices, and introduced himself to the company staff, from tea-boy to chairman. Jagger's psychology was bang-on. It was only

Spring 1973, Ringo instigates a Beatles get-together

sensible for him to have established a rapport with the company since its personnel were, after all, acting on his behalf. Having met the man himself, they were now likely to work all the harder. After all, people tend to work in the record business not because it's well-paid (it isn't), but because they love the music and relish the opportunity of sharing the lift with the occasional star. Even in the supposedly blase rock music industry, meeting Mick Jagger is not just part of the day's work.

There was a second advantage that accrued to Jagger because he'd shown his face at the offices. He had familiarised himself with who did what in the company, and accordingly knew where to direct the appropriate rocket if the Stones' product wasn't being pressed, promoted or distributed properly.

The Beatles had denied themselves these kind of basic business benefits. Just at the very moment when the luminescence was beginning to fade, so that they could have used some marketing assistance, they had ostracised those very people – the press and those in the record industry – who were best-placed to provide it.

The other side of this particular coin is that the Beatles themselves were getting closer together again. Relations between Allen Klein and Lennon, Harrison and Starkey had been ruptured. As far as is known, no-one actually said to them, 'I told you so', but there were many who had only too correctly prophesied how it would all end: with bad feeling, bad grace, and a torrent of writs and counter-writs, with all of them quoting telephone numbers at Klein and vice-versa. (The most absurd of all, which was thrown out of court without delay, was one from Klein, suing McCartney for $34,000,000. He only sued the others for $19,000,000.)

Consequently, this now meant that the four Beatles were all back on the same side of the fence, and the way was open for, if not a Beatle reunion, then at least the resumption of cordial relationships. Certainly, during this period, when they had withdrawn from society, each to his own castle, there was more inter-personal contact than was probably appreciated by the public.

In spring 1973 Ringo extended an invitation to the others to write one song for him for his forthcoming solo album, and then to help him record it. They all readily agreed, and so it was Ringo who proved to be the instigator of a kind of Beatles get-together. At least they once more all appeared on the same album; but although all had turned up at the Sunset Sound studios in Los Angeles, they were never all there simultaneously.

As Nicholas Schaffner says, "The Beatles' collaboration on *Ringo* proved to be just the concoction to wash away the bitter aftertaste that the Beatles' squabbling had left with so many of their fans."

Unabashed by his supposed inferiority, but on the contrary, buoyed by the achievement he felt in bringing them all together, Ringo proceeded to make a magnificent album. In a way, it was a tribute to his particular genius – his eternal good nature and equanimity. People must have felt so squalid, quarrelling in his presence.

So everybody does their best for him. The other three all contribute excellent compositions, and a number of other distinguished guests lend assistance – The Band, Billy Preston, and Harry Nilsson, while Klaus Voorman and Nicky Hopkins again feature.

What the album most obviously conveys is a zestfulness, an unashamed *joie de vivre*. There is no concept as such, although the album gives the appearance of being a stage show, with Ringo's name in lights, and the first and final tracks effectively open and close proceedings.

'Ringo' was brilliant because it was so quintessentially Ringo, but its very success ironically rebounded against him.

The opening song is Lennon's 'I'm The Greatest', which recapitulates the main episodes in Ringo's career in affectionate terms. The song which Paul and Linda had written, 'Six O'Clock' was distinguished by a lovely melody. George, as usual, had been on hand most of the time, and he helped to contribute three songs. His main offering was 'Sunshine Life For Me (Sail Away Raymond)', a sort of update on 'Mother Nature's Son', about a loner who preferred the company of trees to people. There was also 'You And Me (Babe)', the finale-style number, and he also worked with Ringo on the melody for 'Photograph', the track that was issued as the first single from the album, and which became an enormous hit. There were other Ringo compositions, of which the belting 'Oh My My' was the most creditable.

The production had been handled by Richard Perry, whose work was usually noted for its quasi-Spector bombast. On this occasion, he seemed to appreciate exactly what was required: it was pointless to have a strong backing, since the rather tuneless voice would obviously sound absurd in front of lavish orchestral arrangments (as it had done on *Sentimental Journey*), or on the other hand an austere setting, that left the voice to carry the song by itself. However Ringo's vocals did carry a kind of idiosyncratic charm, and so what was needed were arrangements which provided colour and variety to the song, and which somehow complemented Ringo's voice. It was something of a high wire act, but Perry pulled it off – most effectively on a track like 'You're Sixteen', where everything gelled perfectly (even if Nilsson's backing vocals did keep threatening to steal the show).

The album was brilliant because it was so quintessentially Ringo. All those who had assisted – Harrison, Lennon, Nilsson, Perry – understood Ringo's needs, and were determined to fulfil them.

Klaus Voormann contributed a series of lithographs illustrating each song (remember he, with Astrid Kirchherr, had been part of the Hamburg art scene with which the group had socialised in the early '60s, when Stu Sutcliffe was in the band), which formed part of the elaborate and expensive packaging.

Both 'Photograph' and 'You're Sixteen' reached No. 1 in the U.S. singles charts, and 'Oh My My' almost completed the hat-trick. John Lennon sent Ringo a telegram, offering his congratulations and asking the secret of writing hit singles.

Ringo was naturally elated. Since the Beatles had gone their separate ways, he had felt rather isolated. The others were all established songwriters, and could be expected to follow solo careers. That avenue had not intially seemed open to him, and when he had tested the temperature (with *Sentimental Journey* and *Beaucoups Of Blues*) he had found that it wasn't yet safe to go into the water. Hence, he was at a loose end, a redundant millionaire drummer. He could hardly go off and drum for somebody else; once you've been in the Beatles, all other groups seem somehow second-best.

But what could he do? He was not, like John, a natural leader, and was obviously better suited to helping others than to helping himself.

It was the success of what he liked to claim was his first real solo album that helped to resolve such dilemmas. Having already decided to skip *Stardust*, he put his film career in mothballs. He could, after all, be a recording artiste.

The very success of *Ringo* thus rebounded on him, because it persuaded him to shift his career on to a path he was hardly qualified to take. After all, his recording career had

Ringo and Robin Cruickshank, the furniture designer, with whom he launched a range of bespoke furniture and fittings for the home.

worked only under very particular circumstances – the willing participation of the other three, a sympathetic producer, and one or two excellent compositions of his own – and there was no guarantee that they could be re-created, or that the winning formula could be located a second time.

Ringo, however, thought he had cracked it, and there was no-one to suggest otherwise. After *Ringo* his intention became to record one album a year, and he was obviously given full company support to do just that. No longer the poor relation, he took his time recording *Goodnight Vienna*.

The title-track had once again been written by Lennon, but otherwise Ringo had decided to dispense with the services of Harrison and McCartney, lest he be thought to be leaning too heavily on his former colleagues.

This was a ridiculous, and uncharacteristically conceited, mistake for Ringo to make. The whole point is that he always was going to make it with a little help from his friends. The others understood him best. On *Goodnight Vienna*, for example, Ringo had acquired assistance from Elton John, who'd written 'Snookeroo' for him. This was a biographical sketch of a working-class Liverpool lad, but it was pat and unimaginative, and no-one could possibly have identified the character in the song as Ringo.

Although Richard Perry's production was once again reliable, the album was inferior to its predecessor in too many respects. It was no surprise that Ringo's own compositions didn't quite reach the standard he'd earlier set himself, but it was astonishing that he should have renewed pretensions to being a singer; there was no point in him tackling material like Roger Miller's 'Husbands And Wives'. In fact it was because Ringo chose to include more ballad material and fewer strong rockers that the album was noticeably weak.

Nevertheless, there are almost enough worthwhile tracks, and the album-sleeve was good (a parody of the Michael Rennie film, *The Day The Earth Stood Still*). Ringo was to do far worse than this.

In the meantime, though, he launched his own record company, Ring O' Records in April 1975. The name was perfect, but little else about the set-up was right. Certainly, two of the signings were talented professionals: there was David Hentschel, who re-arranged the entire *Ringo* album for synthesiser, and recorded that as *his* debut album – a supreme act of genuflection towards the company boss that was unparalleled in the record industry; and there was Graham Bonnet, one of rock music's notably under-appreciated vocalists. Hentschel subsequently became known through his work as producer for Genesis, and Bonnet joined Ritchie Blackmore's Rainbow for a time; neither, though, found success at Ring O' Records. The label quickly disappeared without being able to claim just one hit, and little more to show that it had ever existed than an initial burst of energy.

Why on earth did Ringo think that Ring O' could ever be a good idea? Was this evidence of delusions of grandeur, or of dilettante dabbling? A tax loss? Certainly, the experience of Apple should have warned the Beatles against such folly. One can naturally appreciate the altruistic desire to assist struggling artists, but there are less risky ways of doing it.

Ringo's other activities during this period included a furniture-designing business with Robin Cruikshank. He had been sporadically involved with this throughout the '70s, but had become less preoccupied with it simply because he was working most frequently on the West Coast of America, and returned to Britain primarily for family visits.

It made sense for him to be working in Los Angeles because most of his friends, like Harry Nilsson and Keith Moon, were there. He helped the latter on his one and only solo album, *Two Sides Of The Moon*, and he and Nilsson worked together on another Apple film, *Son Of Dracula*. This was one of those enterprises which everybody clearly loved making, but which had little to show by way of entertainment as an end product. Nobody seemed to mind, though, and Ringo wryly described the unusual distribution policy that had been evolved for it: "We never put it out here (Britain) or on the Continent. We just put it out in America. We play all the little villages, because if we put it in a town we get slated." He may have been behaving like a dilettante, but he was clearly enjoying himself, and at least he had the recording success which gave him the self-confidence to be able to do it. The week he arrived in the U.K. to launch Ring O', he was back at the top of the U.S. charts, with a *Goodnight Vienna* track, 'No No Song'.

Ringo had appeared towards the end of 1973, at almost exactly the same time as *Band On The Run*, and the release of the two albums gave the solo Beatles a full house; each had now pulled his weight individually, with one excellent album release to his credit. This had been surprising in Ringo's case; by the time it happened, it was no less so in Paul's.

The *Band On The Run* escapade had looked

doomed from the outset. Although Paul had thought it would be interesting to make the album in Nigeria, he had gone there with almost nothing, since two of the band, Denny Seiwell and Henry McCullough, had dropped out virtually at the airport. Their complaint was the usual one – that they didn't like being used as tools of McCartney's trade. It was certainly a problem that had cropped up before (hadn't George, Ringo and John all felt similarly at particular times?). Should rock's boss bass man also be acting as a big boss man?

One couldn't help feeling there were better ways for Seiwell and McCullough to have made their excuses. After all, it wasn't as though McCartney had duped them in any way. Everyone had always known that it was actually his group, and that it was hardly

going to be administered like a parish council. It was only reasonable that Paul should take all the decisions and, indeed, write all the songs because he was the band; whenever he did have democratic lapses, and allow the other band-members to spread their Wings, the results were unsatisfactory.

The walk-out left McCartney with a bundle of problems, since the band now included only himself and Linda and Denny. However, he had been determined that this time he would record an album that would do him justice and so, proving that it's the grit in the oyster that brings out the pearl, he turned a disaster in the making into the greatest triumph of his post-Beatle career. He wrote material while he was in Africa, and painstakingly overdubbed all the extra instruments needed.

For the cover of his 'Band On The Run',
the personalities pictured left were
persuaded to appear following an invitation to lunch.

December, 1973, McCartney is back!

The songs were well-arranged, and both the melodies and the lyrics, which explored the themes of flight, pursuit and freedom, were strong. Indeed, there were moments of lyrical excellence.

And so, in the twelfth month of the year nineteen hundred and seventy-three, it was proclaimed throughout the world: McCartney Is Back.

The track which attracted most immediate attention was the last on Side One, 'Let Me Roll It', which was the final flourish in the protracted, and at times acrimonious, public wrangling of Lennon and McCartney. To the great relief of Beatle fans the world over, that episode was concluded. 'Let Me Roll It' was an affectionate tribute to the works of the Plastic Ono Band, with a vocal track on which McCartney succeeded in sounding more like Lennon than McCartney, and an unmistakeable primal scream at the end. It was brilliant.

One could not help sensing that McCartney had needed to be rigorous in order to achieve his intended effects and that, in trying to produce a gentle parody of Lennon, he had needed to stretch his creative sinews to their utmost to avoid falling flat on his face; obviously, it would be difficult for McCartney to be that disciplined under normal circum-stances, but it seemed as though he should aim more frequently for that kind of concentrated effort.

The album did have its longueurs, notwith-standing the heights which parts of it reached, although its main shortcoming was that it was glaringly weighted in favour of Side One. Those who did persevere with Side Two discovered a track called 'Picasso's Last Words', which was as flatulent an exercise as McCartney had ever concocted. Still, the chorus itself was good (apparently, Dustin Hoffman had suggested to Paul that the last recorded utterance of Pablo Picasso – *"Drink to me, drink to my health/ You know I can't drink any more"* – would make excellent lyrics, at which McCartney composed the tune to go with them there and then), and it was a forgiveable lapse in view of the stunning quality of the overall album.

The public didn't respond immediately, partly because of McCartney's unconvincing recent track record, partly because the album's release coincided with the Christmas holiday period. Sales accumulated during 1974. The album was the first Beatle release ever to be planned properly from a marketing point of view, with an astute strategy mapped out with singles released at judicious intervals, so that it sold consistently well throughout the year. Everyone knows, however, that it didn't sell well because of the marketing plan. It sold well because it was a great record. By the end of the year, it had sold 750,000 copies in Britain, making it EMI's biggest-seller of the decade.

It had taken over three and a half years, but all those who, at the time of the Beatles split, had predicted the greatest personal com-mercial success for McCartney had finally been proved correct. In the U.S. the album sold over five million copies and stayed on the charts for over three years. It marked a real turning-point for McCartney, as Nicholas Schaffner explains in *The Beatles Forever*: "While Paul would soon abandon some of the sense of adventure that helped turn *Band On The Run* into as much of a smash with the critics as with the public, he would never again forget how to make hit records."

So, *Band On The Run* picked up sales after a slow start, while *Ringo* sold enormously well from the beginning. The two between them totally eclipsed John's *Mind Games*, which was released almost concurrently. It was his turn to be class dunce.

McCartney felt a surge of confidence with *Band On The Run* behind him, and worked with renewed vigour throughout 1974. He did a couple of family favours – producing and writing most of an album for his brother, Mike McGear, and recording a song written by his father, 'Walking In The Park With Eloise', credited to the 'Country Hams'.

Wings was brought back to strength with the addition of Jimmy McCulloch, a young, diminutive and exceptionally talented guitarist who had earlier worked with Thunderclap Newman and Stone The Crows, and who would die in 1978, a year after leaving the band. The drummer's stool was filled for a time by Geoff Britton, a U.K. karate expert. His recruitment to the band was potentially very interesting since, whatever the quality of his drumming, it gave the band a different publicity angle. In the event, it soon became clear that his karate activities encroached too much upon the band's schedule, and so he left to be replaced by Joe English, an American whom Wings co-opted while recording in New Orleans.

By this time, Paul had overcome U.S. visa difficulties arising from his drugs convictions in Europe, and so he spent much of the year in America. In Nashville he recorded both the Country Hams single, and also a new one under his own flag, 'Junior's Farm', backed with 'Sally G'. Both sides of the record were hits in the U.S.

This solitary single thus represented the total output of the year from Wings; but McCartney did have the excuse that he'd been busy with other commitments, and in any case a fresh album was hardly necessary while *Band On The Run* was still high on charts throughout the world. Thus, it was not until February 1975 that the band assembled in New Orleans to begin intensive work on a new album.

Venus And Mars was released in the summer of 1975, backed by a massive promotional campaign. This was understandable, because EMI executives must have been delighted when they heard it. The album was exceptionally commercial; McCartney had rediscovered his old flair for composing tracks in a variety of styles, guaranteed to appeal to as wide an audience as possible. One was a '30s-style number, 'You Gave Me The Answer', which McCartney would dedicate to Fred Astaire when he performed it on stage.

This was the album on which McCartney took the stand as a connoisseur of popular art, with the emphasis on 'popular' rather than 'art'. It was a long way from *Sergeant Pepper* and the days when he'd been trying to rouse the others to ever greater heights of artistry. *Venus And Mars* had a sort of commercial television format – everything was easy, nothing was tackled in depth or detail, and lots of areas were covered. Apart from the fact that the album contained a comic book song ('Magneto And Titanium Man'), this attitude was best illustrated by his decision to append his *Crossroads* theme arrangement to the album, a somewhat defiant gesture. It was as though he was saying, "this is popular culture, and that's where I'm at."

Venus And Mars did have its compensations (naturally, since it was a something-for-everybody package). 'Rock Show' was excellent, 'Letting Go' was very good, and there was one sublime, wonderful piece – 'Listen To What The Man Said', which had an authentically smoky New Orleans flavour. Issued as a single, it reached No. 1 in the U.S., and No. 6 in the U.K.

Once the album had safely installed itself at the top of the charts throughout the world, McCartney took his new Wings line-up on tour, playing U.K. dates that would form the first stage of a grand world tour. These were very successful, since the group was in good shape, and Wings had built their own programme – including 'Rock Show', a number that had been written for the specific purpose of becoming a stage number, and one that ensured that Wings' concerts kicked off in fiery style. Many of the loudest roars of approval were, of course, still reserved for the handful of Beatles songs that McCartney felt able to include, but that no longer bothered him as it once would have done. By then, Wings were proving their own pedigree.

The Wings' stage act still hadn't reached the U.S.; that wouldn't happen until the following year. It was George Harrison who became the first ex-Beatle to undertake a Stateside tour of his own.

A lengthy series of concerts had been in his mind since the 1971 Bangla Desh show had generated such an enthusiastic response. Unfortunately, though, it had taken an awful long time to arrange, and when it finally did happen, it did not include any British dates, as had been originally intended.

The wheels were first set properly in motion when Harrison met Ravi Shankar in February, and the latter agreed to be part of the entertainment. The concerts eventually took place in November and December 1974, and obviously stimulated great interest; but in the same way that Harrison had handicapped his recording career, by failing to capitalise soon enough on the success of *All Things Must Pass*, so now he discovered that his stage return had been delayed too long for him to be able to ride on the back of the Bangla Desh triumph. Audiences had changed and, with the '60s that bit much further away, they had become ever more nostalgic for those golden years of the Beatles.

The concerts, then, were not a success. Harrison tended to be in a didactic, sermonising mood – while the audience just wanted to boogie. It was like a culture clash really, East meets West. Most people were not prepared to accept the shows on Harrison's terms. For example, there tended to be restlessness during Ravi Shankar's spots, and in the end it was he who insisted on alterations that would allow the concerts to conform more with the expectations of the audience. His own contribution was reduced from two sets to one opening spot, in which he played briefer and livelier pieces. Then, with some difficulty, he managed to persuade Harrison to deliver more of what the audience wanted from him – viz. Beatle songs. But this was a pyrrhic victory. Harrison had initially eschewed all such considerations, and when he was finally obliged to bow to overwhelming entreaties, he did so with a bad grace. He did begin to include Beatle songs in his set, but invariably tampered with the lyrics, an act of sacrilege that no American audience was going to approve, not even from an ex-Beatle. (In any case, it is surely one thing for George to turn around one of his own compositions, so that it becomes *"While my guitar gently smiles…"*, but quite another for him to alter one of John's – *"In my life/I Love Him more"*.)

The tour featured many top-notch musicians, including Tom Scott and old friend Billy Preston, and in expectation of great success all the shows were filmed and recorded. Things turned so sour that nothing was ever used. The shows seemed to be remembered in positive terms only for the exuberant contributions of Billy Preston.

Matters weren't helped by the fact that Harrison's voice was in bad shape throughout. It had gone croaky in October when he'd arrived in Los Angeles both to rehearse for the concerts and to record a new album. This factor didn't prevent him going ahead with the release of the album, which he wanted in the shops both for the start of the tour and the Christmas holiday period. The record, *Dark Horse*, was a bigger flop than the concerts.

The main problem simply seemed to be one of attitude. Any performer must have in mind, even if only sub-consciously, an audience to whom he is communicating, and presumably must take some precautions, however minimal, to meet the requirements of that audience. Harrison, though, seemed to have broken off diplomatic relations with his; as such, *Dark Horse* simply *seemed* wrong.

Throughout, Harrison was sullen, and preaching at the listener. He had released the album even though, vocally, he had been in no fit state to complete it; the singing is terrible. The cover was ghastly – an old school photograph that he'd messed around with in his humourless fashion. It looked horrible, but there was something else – it betrayed his current philosophy. If, as he claimed at all interviews and press conferences, he was no longer Beatle George, and would have nothing to do with reviving memories of that defunct group, why did he put out a solo album with a cover that was so reminiscent of the famous *Sergeant Pepper* sleeve? (In any case, the trick had been used once too often – Ringo had also used the same kind of idea the previous year for his *Ringo* album.)

There's more yet. The inside cover contained a sub-Desiderata entreaty to critics to judge the album kindly: "The gardener toiled to make his garden fair, most for thy pleasure"; et cetera.

Musicians should know better than humbly to appeal to the good nature of critics. After all, that particular quality is not a necessary qualification for the job, and there are, so I believe, areas where it is felt to be a definite disadvantage.

The final problem was a track called 'Bye Bye Love', George's version of the old Everly Brothers song. He'd written it to suit his own domestic situation. His marriage had collapsed the previous year when his wife Patti had gone off with his best friend, Eric Clapton.

Although George had referred equally to the matter at his Los Angeles press conference in November 1974 ("I'd rather have her with him than with some dope. He's great"), and although it is believed that he himself had accelerated the break-down of the marriage by indulging in a brief liaison with Ringo's wife Maureen (and that was thus the third Beatle marriage in difficulties at this juncture), he nevertheless seemed determined to exact revenge. So, he wrote a new set of unpleasant and self-righteous lyrics to what had once been an attractive song – and then insisted that the objects of his malignity should record it with him. Clapton played guitar, and Patti crooned back-up vocals, while George gleefully sang lines like *"I threw them both out"*. No doubt it was a relief for him to be rid of the pair, but, however resentful George may have felt in the wake of his domestic disharmony, he should hardly have shared his feelings with the public.

The opening track of Side Two of the album was 'Ding Dong', a seasonal song not, for a change, about Christmas, but about the New

Following his split with Patti, George had Clapton and his ex-wife croon back-up vocals to lines like "I threw them both out". George pictured here with current wife, Olivia, who had been working for A & M in Los Angeles.

Year. However, *"Ring out the old, ring in the new"* had another significance for George. On Side One, he had rung out Patti with 'Bye Bye Love', and on Side Two he rang in Olivia, introducing her to his public by using her photograph on the record label. The Mexican-born Olivia Arias had been working for A&M in Los Angeles when George had first come into contact with her. She had subsequently moved to Dark Horse, Harrison's own company, but soon moved in to share George's Friar Park home.

As for the music itself on *Dark Horse* – well, somewhere there were the bones of a good album. The songs were generally well-produced (in a style that now owed less to Spector and was more distinctively Harrison's own), and the guitars frequently sounded good. Songs like 'Simply Shady', 'Dark Horse' itself and 'Far East Man', which he had co-written with Ron Wood, could all have seemed really good – had they been graced with good vocals, and had they appeared in a different context. Basically, it was all too solemn. The album would have benefited enormously from harder work and a lighter touch.

The only other thing to mention is that 'Ding Dong', lifted as the single from this album in time for the holiday season, became the very first Beatle or ex-Beatle single not to chart.

Dark Horse Records had been the third part of George's burst of activity towards the end of 1974.

The contracts of all four Beatles were due to come up for renewal on January 26 1976. Some eighteen months, in advance, therefore, high-level talks began to take place. If, say, George and Ringo wanted to strike custom-label deals for vast sums of money, then they had a useful bargaining-point in their favour: themselves. They could promise to be on their own label as soon as was contractually possible. It was assumed throughout the industry that all four Beatles would be up for grabs, and companies were eager to do what they could to attract any one of them. An ex-Beatle was still considered to be the most prestigious property of all.

This is the background both to Ring O' and to Dark Horse. Certainly, in the case of Dark Horse, Harrison's business manager, Dennis O'Brien, was able to negotiate an exceptionally attractive deal with A&M. Harrison got his own record company; and A&M got the promise of a Beatle from 1976.

Once again it's pertinent to ask, why did George *want* his own record company? Hadn't Apple created enough headaches? However, it can at least be said in his favour that he did take an active role in trying to make the company a viable one.

He signed Bob Purvis and Bill Elliott, a duo who recorded under the name Splinter, produced their debut album for them, and steered the first single from it, 'Costafine Town', into the charts. The song was an attractive one, and that was a very promising beginning. The other initial album release

After leaving Yoko, John slipped away to Los Angeles with Yoko's secretary, May Pang, and "found myself in a sort of mad dream for a year," as he put it.

had inevitably been from Ravi Shankar. No doubt, *Shankar, Family And Friends* was not expected to amass huge sales. Nevertheless, the verdict was that it accumulated disappointingly few. There were also releases from groups called Attitudes and Stairsteps, and also a debut solo album, *Mind Your Own Business* by ex-Wings guitarist Henry McCullough. Dark Horse was undoubtedly a more positive company than Ring O'.

George himself was keen to put *Dark Horse*, the album, behind him as quickly as possible, and so he released a follow-up in what, by current standards, was unusually quick time – about ten months. His eagerness to redeem himself with public and critics alike can be gauged by the fact that he need only have waited another three months and he'd have been able to place the album with his new company. (The fact that he didn't was to have unforeseen consequences.)

In truth, *Extra Texture (Read All About It)* shows little improvement – something it's disappointing to have to say because George was trying very hard, perhaps too hard. The album is long (there's about forty minutes of music) and strings and backing vocals have often been added to the tracks, to give them a commercial bias. Two other features which suggest that George was no longer so scornful of his audience are the opening track, 'You', and the use of 'Legs' Larry Smith, the former drummer with the Bonzo Dog Band, on the closing one, which George had written in tribute to him.

'You' is the song George had composed for Ronnie Spector as a follow-up to 'Try Some, Buy Some'. When the latter failed to click, however, 'You' was never used, and remained unrecorded until George himself dug it out. It was an even stronger song than the original one, and would have suited Ms Spector admirably. On the other hand, while it was

heartening that George should have unearthed 'Legs' Larry (who appears "by permission of Oxfordshire County Council"), the song is not a success, since most of the vocals are lost in the raucous mix; Larry might have had pearls of wisdom to impart, but who could tell? Harrison, now wary of offering sticks for the critics to beat him with, no longer included lyrics sheets with his albums.

Of those tracks where the lyrics are discernible, there are two, 'The Answer's At The End' and 'This Guitar (Can't Keep From Crying)' which again plead plaintively with critics not to judge too severely. In this different context, such pleas are more sympathetic. Very well, then, we will not. *Extra Texture* wasn't really very good musically, and the vocals were still poor, but it did have some appealing qualities, and barely any disagreeable ones.

One of those appealing qualities was the label logo: an Apple core. So it had come to this. At least by releasing it when he did, George had ensured that *Extra Texture* should bear the distinction of being the last album of original material ever to be issued by Apple.

The period had been a particularly strange one for John Lennon. After leaving Yoko and going to Los Angeles (he slipped away with May Pang, Yoko's secretary), he ended up on a long-term binge, leading a riotous, dissipated existence – usually in company with close friends Harry Nilsson, Keith Moon and Ringo. They were more used to this particular lifestyle than he: Nilsson is the rock fraternity's foremost socialite, while living to excess was virtually the only way of life Moon had ever known. To be living in a state of continuous dissolution made quite a change for John; it hadn't been like that since the Beatles had played dates in Hamburg.

Nevertheless, he'd always been a natural for anarchic frivolities, and hardly needed instruction in letting himself go. "I was like a chicken without a head," he told *Rolling Stone*. Most mornings the local papers would carry news reports of Lennon's saturnalian activities. "I'd be waking up drunk in strange places, or reading about myself in the paper, doing extraordinary things, half of which I'd done and half of which I hadn't done. And find myself in a sort of mad dream for a year. You can put it down to which night with which bottle, or which night in which town." (*Rolling Stone*, June 1975.)

It is not difficult to explain this sudden taste for wild intemperance. Lennon's life had been becoming increasingly fraught. The problems over his immigration status, and the possibilities of deportation had been nagging at him continuously for almost two years; his apparently secure relationship with Yoko had broken up; he thought himself in a desperate position – he felt lonely, and he felt

he was getting old. He was also fretful over his comparative lack of record success; his ostensibly jokey congratulatory telegram to Ringo had betrayed actual unease – could he write hit singles any longer? Was he still any good at his job?

Such melancholy thoughts would hardly have been allayed by the experiences he was going through in attempting to record his homage to rock 'n' roll. His concept was an album of non-original material, all classic rock songs of the '50s and early '60s, which would be tackled in the spirit of early, uncompromised rock 'n' roll. "Oldies But Mouldies", he'd thought of calling it. However, the sessions with Phil Spector had hardly been plain sailing.

While Lennon, Nilsson *et al* were residing in a state of temporary madness induced by excessive intake of alcohol, Spector seemed now to be living in his own private hell of real madness. His behaviour had always been wild and erratic, but it had recently developed

Lennon betrayed unease – could he write singles any longer? Was he still any good at his job?

a more sinister edge. He'd been living in isolation for many years – solitary confinement, you might say, since he was well-known to be extremely security-conscious, and to live at the centre of a network of walls and fences and alarms, fortified with his own private arsenal.

He'd taken on virtually no work since the production assistance he'd given to the Beatles and to Lennon and Harrison earlier in the '70s, and Lennon now found him much changed in the interim. For a start, when Lennon and May Pang arrived at his house from the airport, Spector kept them locked in for several hours. When the two of them started work at the Record Plant West, the difficulties just multiplied, and nothing seemed to get done. The more arduous and protracted the sessions became, the less productive they turned out to be. The whole project turned into a nightmare for John. Spector's behaviour was very, very weird.

Confronted with the interminability of the work, Lennon started on another assignment – producing an album called *Pussy Cats* for Harry Nilsson. This fared little better, as the recording sessions became further excuses for carousings and revelry. It was during this time that the most notorious incident in Lennon's "eight-month long weekend", as he referred to it, occurred. He and Nilsson were ejected from the Troubadour Club in Los Angeles for heckling the performers, who happened to be the Smothers Brothers. (Five long years ago, Tommy Smothers had been one of that strange crowd who'd recorded 'Give Peace A Chance' in John's Montreal hotel bedroom.) There was an ensuing melee, a girl was punched, and several press photographers boosted their bank balances.

However, one consolation of the *Pussy Cats* project was that at least Lennon himself was nominally in charge of it, and so by pulling himself together he was able to pull the recording together, by instilling sufficient discipline into the leading personnel to ensure that the album was completed.

The "Oldies But Mouldies" sessions were another matter.

At this time, Bob Mercer was in charge of A&R (Artists and Repertoire) at EMI. He had joined the organisation in 1973, and had tried to restore the company lines of communication with the four Beatles. Thus, he became the EMI representative who had most to do with them until the time when their contracts expired.

In 1974, back in England, he too was perplexed about the Lennon/Spector sessions.

"One had heard, of course, that John was in the studios with Spector, but there had been no official word, and I had never seen any bills come in. Capitol (EMI's U.S. subsidiary) hadn't seen any bills either. So it behoved me to find out if John was actually recording, and, if he was, who was paying his bills – because it really wasn't the Beatles' style to pay their own bills.

"Eventually I discovered that Warner Brothers had been paying them. Spector had persuaded them that he was going to deliver this album to them. How he had actually managed to convince them that this could possibly be their property, God only knows. But whatever the ins and outs of that were – and they would have been intricate, to say the least, if Spector was involved – John *had* been in the studios for quite a long time, the bills had amounted to $90,000, and there wasn't any sign of any tapes."

Mercer explained the situation to Warner Bros., who were duly reimbursed. In the meantime, however, the desultory proceedings at Record Plant West had reached a halt and Lennon headed back East in a state of disillusionment.

Once Lennon had returned to New York from the West Coast, he faced a familiar problem. It was time for him to be in the studios again, working on a new release. All his work over the previous months had, for the moment, come to nothing, and so he would have to start a new album from scratch. Having recruited a familiar nucleus of musicians (Klaus Voormann – bass; Nicky Hopkins – piano; Jim Keltner – drums), John went into New York's Record Plant in August, at which time he had one song written.

The album that grew out of those sessions, *Walls And Bridges*, has always been highly regarded in the U.S., although it failed to make much impact in the U.K. Certainly, it bears the scars of the turmoil of Lennon's personal life, although it tends to be sad and reflective, rather than harrowing. There was a warmth that Lennon's material had been missing for some time, and the tracks included a particularly tender song to Yoko, 'Bless You'. Elsewhere, Lennon's earnest fears about losing his touch and growing old ('Scared', 'Nobody Loves You (When You're Down And Out)') were oft-expressed.

One track, 'Steel And Glass' was very much in the mould of 'How Do You Sleep?' – a quite unambiguous attack on the character of somebody close to Lennon. In this case, few had any doubts that the person referred to was Allen Klein.

The relative success of the singles on each side of the Atlantic illustrate to what extent Lennon had become an American artiste. 'Whatever Gets You Thru The Night' and 'No. 9 Dream' reached Nos. 1 and 9 respectively in the U.S., and Nos. 36 and 23 respectively in the U.K.

Elton John had helped Lennon with the recording of 'Whatever Gets You Thru The Night', after Lennon had helped *him* to lay down material, including a version of 'Lucy In The Sky With Diamonds'. The two had known each other for years, since Elton John had once been a lowly-paid underling in the service of Dick James, the Beatles' publisher.

Their friendship now took on a sudden significance at this stage in Lennon's life. After each had helped out on the other's sessions, Elton asked Lennon if he would perform 'Lucy In The Sky' on stage with him, if 'Whatever Gets You' reached No. 1 in the U.S. charts. Lennon, unduly morose about his present-day hit-making capabilities, agreed. He never dreamed that he'd be called upon to honour his pledge. He'd never had a solo No. 1 before.

So, 'Whatever Gets You' did reach No. 1, and Lennon did go on stage with Elton (it was a special Thanksgiving Day concert at Madison Square Garden) where they performed together – and not only 'Lucy In The Sky'. For an encore, Lennon announced, "We thought we'd do a number by an old estranged fiancé of mine called Paul", and the band surged into a storming version of 'I Saw Her Standing There'.

Lennon had come through a tough year, and had emerged triumphant. "I feel like I've been on Sinbad's voyage, you know, and I've battled all those monsters and I've got back", he explained to *Rolling Stone*. Suddenly, both commercial success and critical laurels were once more flooding in his direction. His appearance on stage had electrified the Madison Square Garden audience, and his gesture towards Paul did not go unnoticed. But there was a more important reason yet why everything suddenly seemed hunky dory again: for the first time that year, he had met Yoko, backstage after the concert (he said he'd never have gone on stage, had he known in advance that she was there; he'd have been too nervous). After a long period of Walls, it

The top UK performers of the '70s (Elton and Bowie) each played a significant part in resuscitating the career and confidence of perhaps the top UK performer of the '60s. Right: John makes a victory sign after winning his fight to stay in the U.S.

was suddenly all Bridges. He didn't move back in with Yoko straightaway – she apparently wanted to make sure that he was genuinely contrite and reformed – but at the beginning of January 1975, he once again took up residence in the Dakota block.

Professionally, two other matters of importance occurred that month. First of all, Lennon accepted an invitation from David Bowie to help him in the recording studio. Like Elton, Bowie was updating Lennon, and doing a new version of 'Across The Universe', on which the original composer agreed to play guitar and sing back-up vocals. Once again, there was an instant rapport in the studio, and Bowie and Lennon collaborated on a new song together, 'Fame', which found its way on to Bowie's *Young Americans* album and which, when issued as a single, reached No. 1 in the U.S. charts. The top U.K. performers of the '70s (Elton and Bowie) had thus each played a significant part in helping to resuscitate both the career and the confidence of perhaps the top U.K. performer of the '60s.

Secondly, the Beatles at last settled their legal differences with each other, and finally dissolved the partnership. Right up to this point, all royalties accruing on Beatles solo product had been paid into a communal Beatles pool. Now, for the first time, the Beatles were legally and financially four independent entities.

At the end of 1974, *Rolling Stone* had printed an article showing how an illegal conspiracy had existed to force Lennon out of the U.S. In that post-Watergate atmosphere, no-one questioned the veracity of the report and from that moment on Lennon was winning every stage of his legal battle to remain in the U.S. John's joy was completed in February with the news that Yoko was pregnant, and he immediately began to cut

back on his work schedule in order to help her through her confinement.

Only one cloud remained in the sky: the vexed question of the rock 'n' roll album. John thought he had overcome all the problems, but there was one hurdle left.

Once the tapes had been released, he was able to get on with the job, and completed recording the album in New York. He took care to indicate on the sleeve that one-third of the material had been recorded by Phil Spector over a four-month period, and two-thirds had been recorded by Lennon himself in just four days. Since he felt that the old title had been somewhat unlucky, he called the album quite simply, *Rock 'n' Roll*.

In order to emphasise that the recordings were intended to have a period feel to them, Lennon used a cover shot of himself in his Hamburg days as a greasy rocker. The album was excellent, if only because it showed how affectionately Lennon regarded his rock 'n' roll heritage.

The difficulty that had arisen was an entirely fresh one. Some years earlier, Lennon had been sued by Morris Levy, Chuck Berry's publisher, for having appropriated lines from Berry's 'You Can't Catch Me' and used them in the *Abbey Road* track, 'Come Together'. The implied charge of plagiarism was grossly unfair, since Lennon had made no attempt to disguise the provenance of the lyrics, and had clearly included them as a kind of tribute.

In the event, Levy agreed to drop the charges once Lennon had offered to include two Chuck Berry compositions – 'You Can't Catch Me' and 'Sweet Little Sixteen' – on a future album.

Having therefore recorded the songs, Lennon mailed Levy an early tape of the sessions, as evidence that he had carried out his promise. Levy then produced an album from this tape, and started marketing it under the title

'Roots' as a television mail-order offer. It was as a result of this that EMI/Capitol issued *Rock 'n' Roll* so swiftly on the heels of *Walls And Bridges*. (The albums were issued within five months of each other.)

At this point, Lennon decided that he'd been conned and cheated by record industry wheeler-dealers once too often. A court injunction was brought against Levy to prevent him selling the record, and a year later Lennon won a court judgement against him, as a result of which Levy was told to pay $45,000 to cover damages he might have inflicted on Lennon's reputation.

"Roots" happened to be of some interest to the ardent Beatle fan, since it did include two tracks, 'Be My Baby' and 'Angel Baby', which were omitted from the authorised album. In the event, *Rock 'n' Roll* sold disappointingly, which perhaps wasn't surprising, since the whole intention of the album had been to swim vigorously against the contemporary tide.

There was, thankfully, no miscarriage for Yoko this time, and a son, Sean Ono, was born on October 9 1975 – also John's 35th birthday. His cup was overflowing. Two days earlier the U.S. Court of Appeals had overturned the order to deport him. Everything had come right over the past year. "I feel", said John, "higher than the Empire State building."

CHAPTER

7

Established Identities

The contracts which Allen Klein had re-negotiated on the Beatles' behalf expired on January 26 1976. Notwithstanding all the frantic behind-the-scenes negotiations that had been in progress for the previous eighteen months – "everybody was talking to everybody", as Bob Mercer put it – the only one of the four committed to a definite course of action was George, who had agreed to sign himself to his own A&M-backed Dark Horse label.

Broadly, the position was this. On the one hand, the company was able to claim possession of the Beatles' catalogue in perpetuity; and as long as the individual ex-Beatles stayed with the company, they were better able to control the disposition of that catalogue. However, there was much to EMI's disadvantage – the most obvious of which was that, having been with the company throughout, the four knew it inside out (or thought they knew it).

Finally, it was perhaps too much to expect any one company to afford the sort of deals to which the individual Beatles now felt

January, 1976, the EMI-Beatles bond is broken

themselves entitled. In the event, EMI made one exception: Paul McCartney received the kind of offer that even rock stars find hard to refuse; although since he was, in strict commercial terms, the safest bet of the four, this was hardly reckless extravagance on EMI's part, more a calculated gamble. Although he signed with Columbia for the U.S. and Canada, McCartney chose to stay with EMI for the rest of the world. Ringo also opted for a dual arrangement, joining Atlantic for the North American territories, and Polydor elsewhere. John, having fulfilled all his contractual obligations, determined not to take on any more.

Thus, the EMI–Beatles bond was broken. Ever since the break-up EMI had refrained from any actions which might jeopardise their chances of re-signing the four in 1976. Now that moment had come and gone, there was no longer any particular need to heed their wishes in respect of their catalogue (although they were still careful not to upset McCartney). EMI could begin to examine the question of recycling the Beatles.

There are those who consider such exploitation to be wholly unethical. Bob Mercer takes the opposite view. "It's a catalogue, and you own it. You can't just let it sit there and do nothing. Contractually, the Beatles didn't have the right to say we couldn't do it, and commercially we had a need to do it.

"People who complain about that sort of thing are really pissing in the wind. If a new compilation is issued, no one is required to buy it. As long as some legitimate thought has gone into it, it's not a marketing rip-off, it's a marketing technique, and to my mind a justifiable one."

EMI's immediate strategy combined speed with caution. In February 1976 they simply re-promoted every one of the Beatles' singles. They were not, they insisted, re-issuing them, since they had never been out of catalogue. Many people had probably never realised this so the effect was as striking as if they had been re-issued; all the singles returned to the U.K. Top 100 best-sellers, which therefore gave the Beatles virtually one-quarter of the entire chart. There had been twenty-two U.K. singles issued during the lifetime of the Beatles, and to these EMI had thoughtfully added a new one, 'Yesterday', which climbed straight into the Top 10. John approved of the idea of re-promoting all the 45s in their original form, and Paul liked the idea of issuing 'Yesterday' for the first time. Everyone was happy.

The next moves from the company were more controversial. A double-album compilation, *Rock 'n' Roll Music*, was issued during the summer. In line with EMI policy, the Beatles had been invited to offer their thoughts, and John and Ringo had contributed ideas. There was therefore nothing wrong with the selection of material. However, the cover, which had been designed by Capitol in the U.S., was a disgrace.

The graphics had been conceived in terms of 'rock 'n' roll' rather than 'the Beatles', and illustrated artefacts of '50s U.S. culture – i.e. they portrayed the atmosphere in which the original music had been created but had nothing at all to do with the Beatles. Indeed, it represented those very cultural icons that the Beatles had thankfully toppled. It could not, in fact, have been less appropriate.

A tacky cover is hardly an unusual occurrence in the record business, but it *was* unprecedented for the Beatles and it did cause a furore. Ringo told Paul Gambaccini in *Rolling Stone*: "It made us look cheap and we never were cheap. When we worked, we spent as much time on the cover as on the tracks. John even said he'd do a new cover, but they refused. I mean, John has more imagination than all those people at Capitol put together." EMI (UK) were equally incensed, but had to go along with releasing the compilation because their U.S. company had pulled the rug from under them. It was nevertheless as a result of the *Rock 'n' Roll Music* débâcle that an internal group was formed at EMI (UK) specifically to coordinate the compilation and release of Beatles' material.

Subsequent albums were indeed less offensive. There was another compilation, *Love Songs* (the natural companion-piece to *Rock 'n' Roll Music*) released in November 1977, although the sleeve-design in that case was hardly wonderful either.

In fact, no Beatle compilation, however well-conceived, was likely to be greeted with loud hosannas. EMI had set themselves a thankless task. There was a finite amount of publicly-available Beatles material, and beyond a certain point there was little sense in re-shuffling the songs. Ordinarily, compilations of an artist's material might serve the valuable function of weeding out the dross; with the Beatles, there was simply no dross to weed out.

A more interesting project, therefore, was the release of live recordings from the Hollywood Bowl concerts of 1964 and 1965. There had never previously been a live Beatles album. George Martin diligently prepared the tapes for release, bringing the sound quality up to scratch for the late '70s. This too was a venture that Lennon concerned himself with, and the results were excellent – and emphatically proved that behind that barrage of screaming, the Beatles really had been pumping out something worthwhile.

It was widely considered that sales of *The Beatles At The Hollywood Bowl* had been disappointing. In fact, when judged against the size of the promotional budget (this was

the first-ever Beatles album to be TV-advertised), they were disastrous. EMI has since tried nothing similar. There was, however, a parallel release organised by Allan Williams, briefly manager of the Beatles in their embryonic days, who arranged for the belated release of a tape he had procured of the Beatles playing at the Star Club, Hamburg, late in 1962. The four Beatles jointly, but vainly, tried to prevent its release. By this time the Beatles, recidivist litigants, had no doubt exhausted judicial patience.

The double-album, *Live At The Star Club, in Hamburg, Germany 1962*, was duly released. Many critics welcomed it, pointing out that it featured songs that the group had not previously recorded. In reality, it was of minimal interest. The sound quality was appalling, and the recording didn't even derive from their most frenetic Hamburg days. On the contrary, it was made at their last engagement there, which had been undertaken only to fulfil contractual obligations, and when their EMI recording career was already under way.

Such renewed interest in Beatles' recordings coincided with a period when progress reports on the individual careers of the four thus far were being delivered via the release of compilation albums. John was first off the blocks with *Shaved Fish (Collectable Lennon)*. This was particularly timely. It was released in October 1975, and coincided with the birth of Sean, the event which had precipitated John's decision to withdraw from professional activities for a period. *Shaved Fish* thus neatly wrapped up that part (the overwhelming part, as it turned out) of his solo career.

Shaved Fish included eleven Lennon/Plastic Ono Band songs issued as singles, but omitted the last one, 'Stand By Me', from *Rock 'n' Roll*. It was thus a straightforward

PAUL McCARTNEY

For their different reasons, John and George had felt the more frustrated within the Beatles and consequently felt a keener sense of relief when it had all been concluded, however messily. Paul reacted differently. Like John, he had little actually to prove. No one doubted his ability to survive as a solo artist. Yet, the effect of the split was shattering; he'd been eager to keep the show on the road and hence he was initially disorientated by its demise. Nor was he able, for some considerable time, to attain a creative plateau of his own.

If Paul dabbled in Eastern mysticism, experimented with mind expanding drugs, and was a major force in changing the course of contemporary rock, it was only when he put all this behind him, settled into a comparatively cosy, bourgeois life-style with Linda, and stopped striking attitudes and

being self-consciously calculating that his career took off once more.

Paul needed an audience, and in February 1972 he began a series of concerts with Wings that were conducted with utmost secrecy so that they could develop and make close contact with audiences at small venues away from the glare of too much publicity. These may have been relatively low-key, warm-up gigs by comparison with what was to follow,

but were of crucial importance. The line-up included Linda on keyboards, Denny Laine on guitar, and Denny Seiwell on drums.

It all happened for Paul in 1973. He had his own television special; Wings undertook their first full-length tour in Britain; he recorded the theme music for *Live And Let Die* and he went to Nigeria to record *Band On The Run*. Following his 1975/'76 world tour, Paul never looked back.

The man most likely to . . .

collection, and it was difficult to explain why it seemed disappointing. Perhaps it was because John's music had been so diverse. Tracks like 'Mother' and 'Woman Is The Nigger Of The World' only seemed right in their original contexts.

Nevertheless, the album sold encouragingly, which is more than can be said for *Blast From Your Past*, a premature compilation from Ringo. Released just a few weeks after *Shaved Fish*, it seemed a rushed, commercial undertaking – as indeed, it probably was, since Ringo had no other product to promote that Christmas. At five tracks a side, it seemed to offer the bare minimum.

Shaved Fish and *Blast From Your Past* were the very last releases on the Apple label. After January 26, 1976, there was no longer any point in retaining it. The reason why Ringo had rushed *Blast From Your Past* thus became clear. At least he had been able to control its release. EMI soon decided to do a compilation themselves for George Harrison,

a project from which he dissociated himself completely. *The Best Of George Harrison* contained one side of his efforts as a Beatle, and one side of solo undertakings, and thus enabled one to make interesting comparisons; certainly, the solo work held its own even when juxtaposed with the Beatles material. Harrison's disapproval was no doubt at least partly due to the fact that Capitol's half-and-half arrangement (no doubt devised for commercial reasons) made it look as though he was the only one of the four with insufficient clout as a solo artist to warrant a 'Greatest Hits' comprised entirely of his own work.

Wings Greatest did not materialise until 1978, by which time McCartney, who had assembled the compilation himself, had had ample time to compile a catalogue of hits, and was able to include on it 'Mull Of Kintyre', which the year before had become the U.K.'s top-selling single of all time. Although the selection of tracks couldn't

Paul at his Campbeltown studio in Scotland conducting members of the Campbeltown Pipe Band in 'Mull of Kintyre', the top-selling UK single of all time.

have been easy – of necessity much material had to be excluded – the album nevertheless betrayed signs of amnesia on Paul's part. He had passed over lesser triumphs like 'Helen Wheels', but if one-time embarrassments like 'Give Ireland Back To The Irish' and 'Mary Had A Little Lamb' were omitted, so too were highly reputable tracks like 'C Moon', 'Girl's School' and 'Sally G'. Neither was 'Listen To What The Man Said' included – and whether judged by a commercial or a critical yardstick, that had to be one of Wings' greatest. So was Paul carefully leaving himself plenty of options for a Volume 2? Or is it simply that collections of an artist's work are best assembled by someone other than the artist himself?

The sum of all this is that none of the four compilations was wholly satisfactory. Although there is no common factor to explain this, it is noticeable that this marked the beginning of a difficult stage of their solo careers. With EMI beginning to recycle the Beatles' material nostalgia for the group was suddenly blossoming. The four often found present efforts rendered negligible by past achievements – indeed, predetermined to such a fate. Small wonder that Lennon, the only one not engaged upon solo undertakings, should have been the only one to show consistent interest in the development of the Beatles legend, or that, George, for example, should have found his confidence at a low ebb during the second half of the 70s.

In 1976, just when it seemed that the myriad legal complexities to which the dissolution of the Beatles had given birth, had been finally resolved, George Harrison found himself in court on two matters on his own account. Bright Tunes Publishing sued him over alleged copyright infringement, and A&M Records took legal action against him, on the grounds that he had failed to deliver the solo album that he contractually owed him.

The dispute surrounding 'My Sweet Lord', which to many people had seemed to be too close for comfort to the old Chiffons' hit 'He's So Fine', had dragged on for some considerable time. Once legal action had been instigated, there had been an initial hearing, at which it had been suggested that the songs were similar, and that possibly the two parties could agree between themselves some method of dividing the royalties. No doubt had Ronnie Mack, the composer of 'He's So Fine' still been alive, everything could have been resolved without rancour at that point. However, he wasn't, there was no longer any personal ownership of the copyright, and hence the case was pursued to its bitter end.

After a lengthy court case in August 1976, during which numerous witnesses were summoned, the judge, Richard Owen, concluded that 'He's So Fine' and 'My Sweet Lord' were the same song, that Harrison had been guilty of "unconscious plagiarism", and that therefore composition royalties on the song should be made over to Bright Tunes.

No-one in the U.S. seemed especially surprised by this verdict. 'He's So Fine' had been a memorable No. 1 back in 1963, and disc-jockeys, amongst others, had constantly cited the song as the clear inspiration of 'My Sweet Lord'. In the U.K., where 'He's So Fine' had had only limited, ephemeral impact, there had been little comment on the similarity. There was thus mild surprise when Harrison lost the case, although little attention was paid to the court verdict. Presumably it was felt that Harrison had riches enough not to worry about the pecuniary penalties, and that his reputation, after all that time, hardly rested on just that one song. There was little public sympathy for Harrison, who was therefore left to nurse a deep sense of injustice by himself.

GEORGE HARRISON

George made perhaps the most natural progression from being a Beatle. His artistic development had been both fostered and stunted by working in close proximity to Lennon and McCartney: fostered because the competitive atmosphere encouraged him to write his own songs; stunted because he was frequently not given the chance to display his emerging talents.

There was notable constancy in George's lifestyle following the disintegration of the group: no immediate change of partner (being already married to Patti, no new personal influence arose); and his interest in all things Eastern also survived the split to become the inspiration of his hugely successful Bangla Desh concert, involving leading rock artists and, of course, Ravi Shankar.

Given the limitations of his position within the Beatles, George had emerged with a veritable bank of musical material which he put to tremendous effect in *All Things Must Pass*, though his immediate career suffered from putting all his eggs in this one basket.

He must have found it difficult striving for spiritual goals while simultaneously being a famous millionaire, and the quandry was well expressed on the cover of his 1973 release *Living In The Material World*. It showed holy symbols and Sri Krishna messages alongside his co-musicians enjoying a hearty repast, while the longest limousine in the world awaited their convenience. The album was also very ambiguous in its allegiances, though much of the music itself was exceptionally fine. Unfortunately the concensus was that the concept was ill-timed, almost old-fashioned in its theme. The fact was that no one of the Beatles could any longer write the rules. The game itself had changed, and at this point George had failed to assess his position in it. This was never more apparent than in his unsuccessful tour of the US in 1974. Two law suits, another unsuccessful album, and a serious bout of hepititis later, George issued *33⅓*, a genuine improvement though still short of his best. He followed this with a period of temporary retirement, great success with the Monty Python team, and in 1979, *George Harrison*, his most successful album since *All Things Must Pass*.

The dark horse . . .

In fact, within the context of rock music, it was an unjust decision; it is a great pity it cannot be reversed. Harrison had vainly tried to argue that if the song was based on anything, it was 'Oh! Happy Day'. There is no reason to doubt his word in this. After all, it makes sense, since the version of the song by the Edwin Hawkins Singers had been a No. 2 hit in Britain only the year before 'My Sweet Lord' was composed. One ethno-musicologist called to give evidence at the hearing confirmed that both 'He's So Fine' and 'My Sweet Lord' were derived from a common source – 'Oh! Happy Day'; and that, a nineteenth-century gospel song was in the public domain.

The New York court clearly understood nothing of rock 'n' roll, or gospel, or popular music in general. *Rolling Stone* pointed out that Judge Owen was a classically-trained musician who composed operas in his spare time. The verdict was simply based on the fact that the three bars of music which accompanied the title refrain were the same. The notations, identical ones, were displayed in court on a blackboard. "Don't you agree," the judge asked one of the witnesses, "that this is the same song?" "That's not a song," he replied, referring to the blackboard, "that's a riff."

Indeed. Previously thousands of pop/rock songs had approximated closely to thousands of others, and there had been scarcely any litigation. Usually, there had been something which made a particular recording distinctive. In the case of 'My Sweet Lord' innumerable factors ensured that stylistically the two songs did not resemble each other at all.

It would have been interesting for rock music in general had that become a genuine test case, but in fact no-one has since taken comparable action over copyright infringement, even though artists have continued to be inspired, unconsciously or consciously, by existing compositions. The most blatant recent case concerned a song called 'Start!' by the Jam, which reached No. 1 in the U.K., and therefore attained a prominence which might have rendered it liable to legal action. The song it was clearly modelled on (some of the chords were identical) was, irony of ironies, George Harrison's Beatles song, 'Taxman'.

This was also a matter for debate on radio stations. In contrast to the way he had himself been treated, however, Harrison declined to take legal action, or even to make public comment. As the ex-Beatle most evidently preoccupied with spiritual concerns, he has sometimes been upbraided for displaying excessive symptoms of worldliness in his business dealings. (It is not a criticism with which this author has particular sympathy, but it is one that has been frequently heard. One occasion which does come to mind is when he withdrew permission for two of his songs to be used in the *John, Paul, George, Ringo . . . And Bert* stage show. That *had* to be either malicious or misguided; Willy Russell's play, after all, was a well-written, entertaining, and largely respectful one.) His restraint in the 'Start!' affair showed that he could exercise greater generosity of spirit than a grudging press frequently allowed.

The other legal difficulty was settled less distastefully. Having released *Extra Texture* the previous autumn, George had begun work on his next album early in the new year in order to have it ready to deliver to A&M by the July 26 deadline stipulated in his lucrative new contract. However, he was laid low with a bout of hepatitis (and, indeed, was very poorly at one point), and the illness inevitably wrecked the recording schedule.

On September 28, therefore, A&M filed a

George at the Silverstone race track watching the practice-runs for the British Grand Prix.

himself had lately seemed more a financial liability than asset (A&M could hardly have failed to notice the disappointing sales for both *Dark Horse* and *Extra Texture*) and his credibility as a company flagship evaporated along with his commercial standing.

The new album, titled *33⅓* to indicate both the speed at which it should be played and Harrison's age at the time he had been recording it, was released in November 1976. It was a genuine improvement, and sold encouragingly.

Despite the rift with A&M, one of the tracks, 'Learning How To Love You', was dedicated to A&M founder and vice-president, Herb Alpert. This relatively minor point was illustrative of a new spirit: George no longer seemed embittered and resentful; the solemn sermonising had disappeared, and the album seemed altogether more convincing as a result. His spiritual convictions no longer seemed to be cramping his style, but affording him a generous and open heart.

An excellent production and frequently inspired guitar work were amongst the other positive qualities which the album could boast. However encouraging, though, the album was still a long way short of his best. The songs couldn't really be classed as first-rate compositions, even though several did have their interesting features: 'Pure Smokey' (like 'Ooh Baby' from the previous album) was dedicated to Smokey Robinson, one of George's favourite singers, and 'Crackerbox Palace', one of the better tracks, had taken its title from the home of Lord Buckley, the humorist celebrated for his hip religion monologues who had died in New York in 1960. There was a surprising non-original, Cole Porter's 'True Love' (sung by Bing Crosby in *High Society*), which was handled in quite sprightly fashion; "It's a bit slow the way Bing does it," explained George.

$10 million suit against him, alleging that Harrison had broken the terms of his contract by failing to deliver his album on time. It was all settled amicably enough; the Dark Horse-A&M contract was simply annulled, and Harrison shunted both himself and his label over to Warner Bros, where Derek Taylor, his old friend (and the Beatles' one-time press agent) held an executive position.

Since an inability to meet the deadlines is as common in the recording business as it is in publishing, and since no one could reasonably have failed to sympathise with Harrison's indisposition, it was believed throughout the industry that A&M were not really worried about the lateness of the album at all. They simply wanted an excuse to get out of the Dark Horse contract, having spent over $2.5 million promoting the company's albums in the first place, and having seen precious little return for their investment. Further, Harrison

'This Song' was an ironic comment upon the 'My Sweet Lord' case (*"This song came to me/Quite unknowingly"*). Eric Idle tossed in a few comments in one of his Monty Python voices, and also helped George with promotional films to accompany three of the tracks; the two had met at the Hollywood premiere of *Monty Python And The Holy Grail*, and became firm friends almost immediately.

33⅓ made little headway in the U.K., but it did help to restore George to favour in the U.S. Having spent some time lending personal assistance to the U.S. promotional campaign, George then relaxed for a time. A whole year, in fact, since he did nothing during 1977.

Like Lennon, he felt an inescapable need to go into temporary retirement. Each had spent a significant part of the '70s being hounded through a succession of courts in a variety of cases, and probably only those who have experienced it can appreciate how mentally fatiguing such incessant pressure is. George also probably felt in need of an artistic respite and, having clawed his way back to higher ground with *33⅓*, felt that this was now the opportunity to relax, to allow his frayed creative faculties time to be refreshed. It was, in any case, 1977: The Year Of The Punk, and like other prominent symbols of rock's status quo Harrison would have realised that it would not be imprudent to go to ground at that point.

He found little difficulty in deriving immense satisfaction from his sabbatical. He indulged his passion for watching motor racing, and numbered drivers like Jackie Stewart, as well as motor-cycling star Barry Sheene, amongst his close friends. His domestic harmony blossomed as his relationship with Olivia Arias developed smoothly. They finally got married on September 8, 1978, just five weeks after the birth of their son, Dhani.

In recent years George has seemed more placid and secure, and less tormented and uptight. He has conferred numerous acts of kindness on friends, associates and charities, few of which are ever usually hinted at in the press. John Blake, in the *Evening News*, related that he'd given three large precious rubies to the landlady of his local pub as a birthday present. Harrison seemed to have laid the demons of Beatlemania, and finally to have emerged in a state of spiritual contentment.

His friendship with Eric Idle yielded surprising results. Firstly, he made a brief guest appearance in a television film devised by Idle, *The Rutles*, which was an effective spoof of the Beatles legend; George rejoiced that the whole history was being satirically deflated.

Of much more importance, however, was his involvement in *Life Of Brian*, the Monty Python film which had run into financial difficulties in 1979 when Lord Grade (head of EMI, the company making the film) had withdrawn his backing since he feared it would prove blasphemous. The production was thus stymied. Harrison, in an unfamiliar role as the entire U.S. cavalry, came to the rescue by writing out a cheque for £2 million to enable the film to be completed. The film, in which Harrison made another guest appearance, proved overwhelmingly successful, and recovered its costs many times over. As a result, Idle and Harrison created Handmade Films, with the specific intentions of ensuring that all Pythonesque ideas could be used to their maximum effect with minimum hassle, and that the completed films could get proper distribution. The company thus started off with a 100% success record, and maintained it by picking up the distribution rights to *The Long Good Friday*,

In recent years George would seem to have resolved his
insecurities, laid the demons of Beatlemania and emerged
in a state of spiritual contentment.

1976-'80, George at a "leisurely" pace...

an excellent British thriller directed by John MacKenzie which had been shunned by the major distributors. A new Handmade film for which Harrison had written the title music, *Time Bandits*, starring Ralph Richardson, David Warner and Shelley Duvall, and directed by Terry Gilliam from a script by himself and Michael Palin, opened in London in July 1981. The next major concern of the company would be another full-scale Python film.

Harrison's own career, meanwhile, was pursued at a stately pace, with none of the tensions that had accompanied it in the mid-'70s. He released, in fact, only two albums in the five years from 1976-80 – *33⅓* and *George Harrison*, released in February 1979. Its baldly unambitious title notwithstanding, *George Harrison* is his most successful album since *All Things Must Pass*, and would probably have sold in its millions had it arrived at the beginning rather than the end of the decade. Nevertheless it should help restore Harrison's erstwhile pre-eminence.

The album is more melodic than any of the others, Harrison sings more effectively, and the guitar parts are invariably excellent. In requesting the assistance of a Warner's staff producer, Harrison had displayed that essential touch of humility – the absence of which had given birth to many of the difficulties the four had encountered. Russ Titelman, who co-produced, thus became the only person apart from Phil Spector to serve such an important function on one of George's albums. The co-production arrangement proved wholly beneficial.

Right from the joyous first track, 'Love Comes To Everyone', the album was characterised by many of the positive qualities (consistency, professionalism, confidence, ebullience) that had graced Beatles' recordings. 'Blow Away' in particular would have been a huge U.K. hit, had the Beatles' sheen not become dulled by then. (In the U.S., inevitably, the album enjoyed considerable, if not exceptional, success.) The standard of musicianship was very high, and there was a light, jazzy feel to several tracks, including 'Not Guilty', a song which, as lines like *"I won't upset the apple-cart"* suggested, had been written back in 1969, but then forgotten. In 'Faster', Harrison had set himself the task of writing a song about the Grand Prix circuit, and had succeeded admirably. (Royalties on the song were donated to the Gunnar Nilsson Charity Fund for cancer.) 'Soft-Hearted Hana' showed a facility for switching style and mood that, again, rendered comparisons with the Beatles not at all invidious. Harrison undeniably lacks the lyrical capabilities that Lennon consistently, and McCartney intermittently, displayed – but he had has his own strengths which he has used to good advantage here. *George Harrison* can lay claim to being one of the best Beatle solo efforts.

A different project to which he directed his energies was a putative autobiography, which included memorabilia such as original word-sheets of his songs, and which was presented in a leather-bound, limited (semi-private, in effect) edition, at a retail cost of £148. (The individual Beatles had always insisted that their products were packaged elaborately, but this was ridiculous.)

George may have found the title, *I, Me, Mine* beautifully apposite, but others thought that the egotism had been carried too far. John Lennon believed that several personalities, notably himself, had been granted insufficient credit by George. "His book says, by glaring omission, that my influence on his life is absolutely zilch and nil. In his book, which is purportedly this clarity of vision of his influence on each song he wrote, he remembers every two-bit sax player or guitarist he met in subsequent years. I'm not in the book. I'm slightly resentful." (*Playboy*, January 1981.)

Immediately he saw these comments (in common with most magazines, *Playboy* is printed and published some weeks before its stated date of issue), George wrote a song by way of reply. What this would have said will probably never been known, since in the wake of John's murder, George wrote a completely fresh lyric to the tune, so that it became a song of tribute, and was one of the tracks included on his 1981 album, *Somewhere In England*.

Whatever George's response may have been, it's strange that after all that time he should still have been so concerned about projecting his own image. Even the most curmudgeonly critic could not deny that his solo career had had its moments, and one would have supposed that he'd crawled from under John's shadow a long time ago. For the fact that it represented a step backwards at a time when his music was again moving forwards, as well as for the necessarily esoteric nature of such an absurdly-budgeted project, *I, Me, Mine* was an ill-starred enterprise.

Harrison's *Somewhere In England* was the first Beatle album to appear after Lennon's death, and it included not only a dedication to him, but also the song George had written (or, re-written) in tribute. 'All Those Years Ago' was virtually a Beatles recording, since it featured Ringo and Paul and Linda; further, George Martin had assisted on the production. The words were sincere and heartfelt, the song itself one of Harrison's best solo compositions. It wasn't merely as a result of the exhaustive publicity given to the recording of the song that, when issued as a single, it shot into the Top 10 on both sides of the Atlantic.

The rest of the album was painstakingly prepared, and much of it very effective. There was the usually excellent guitar work to accompany tracks concerned with, for example, the soullessness of the disco dance-floor ('Unconsciousness Rules'), or the lemming-like attitudes of the record industry ('Blood From A Clone'). Not that all Harrison's preoccupations were so humdrum. It was only characteristic of him to embrace more universal themes; one track was called 'Save The World', and probably only he could have composed a song entitled 'Like Itself'.

In addition, there were a couple of old Hoagy Carmichael numbers, 'Baltimore Oriole' and 'Hong Kong Blues', but they probably could have benefited from stronger vocals. In fact, for all its merits, the album made one realise anew how interlocking had been the strengths of the four Beatles. Many of the songs on *Somewhere In England* would have fitted impressively on to a Beatles album; when placed consecutively, however, Harrison's limitations as a vocalist became more clearly exposed. The album obviously, inevitably, lacked the diversity and scope that had characterised the music of the Beatles.

The expiry of the Beatles' EMI contracts occurred at a propitious time for Ringo, given that he had only lately resoundingly established his commercial credibility with *Ringo* and *Goodnight Vienna*. He could therefore look forward to the same kind of lucrative offer that the other three would expect; he didn't, however, get it from EMI.

"I think he was pissed off with that," said Bob Mercer. "I think that despite the much-publicised problems they'd had with EMI, there was nevertheless a certain amount of loyalty to the company – and a certain amount of Englishness too. When Ringo got an offer from EMI that was substantially less

Ringo, having long been fascinated
by photography, decided to direct *Born To Boogie*,
the contemporary substitute for '60s Beatlemania

than that being offered by other companies, he felt slighted.

"My only response was, we know what you sell, better than anyone else. His feeling was (and it happened to a degree with all of them) that EMI should make a deal with them that compensated for the deals they'd had in the past. Whether that was a philosophy with which I had had any sympathy was neither here nor there – that wasn't the reality. The deals they'd had in the past were the deals they'd had in the past. The deals they had in the future couldn't be influenced by them. If Polygram (the international conglomerate that owns Polydor), or WEA decides to pay more than the market price for one of the Beatles as a flagship, then that's their decision."

So, Ringo parted company with EMI, and signed with an American concern for the U.S. and Canada, and a European conglomerate for Europe and the rest of the world. The fact that his career nosedived almost immediately is not necessarily a result of his label-switch.

The Polydor deal was signed in March 1976, and Ringo's debut album for them, *Ringo's Rotogravure*, duly arrived in September, complete with a back-cover photograph of the graffiti'd front door of the Apple offices in Savile Row; the Beatles, you see, still meant a lot to Ringo. If the cover evoked golden memories, however, the record unfortunately didn't.

Ringo had revived Plan (A) for the occasion. This stipulated the inclusion of one new composition from each of the other three, but the effect was not nearly so invigorating as it had been on *Ringo*. John's song, 'Cookin'', showed his inventiveness to be at an unusually low ebb; Paul's 'Pure Gold' wasn't at all Ringo-type material, and George's 'I'll Still Love You' had actually been written some years earlier for Cilla Black, but had been

returned by her, unused. In addition, Eric Clapton had contributed a lightweight composition. For once, Ringo's friends were finding it difficult to keep him afloat.

The main reason was the wholly unsympathetic production, by Arif Mardin. He would have been quite at home arranging sessions for Aretha Franklin and Atlantic's other soul singers, but floundered when he tried to apply similar techniques to a Ringo recording session.

If Atlantic was hardly a natural home for Ringo, it would be misleading to blame the company for that. Ringo was by now in a position to exercise full control over his own career, and so all the mistakes would have been his. Neither would the album have been promoted or marketed any less intensively by this company than by any other. In this respect, the four individual Beatles had reached an interesting commercial point by this time; unlike virtually all other rock acts their records sold simply on the strength of the product. If the album was good, it sold well, and if not, it sold disappointingly.

What had probably gone wrong with *Ringo's Rotogravure* was that Ringo was simply flattered that someone like Mardin should be acting as producer for someone like him. Mardin did Ringo the further honour of treating him just like any other of his charges – which was, of course, a cardinal error. Ringo's records worked only when they sounded distinctly like Ringo. But Ringo, having chosen an inappropriate producer, compounded his difficulties by selecting inappropriate material. The result was an anonymous and lacklustre album. Even so, Ringo's penance seemed somewhat extreme when he had his head shaved shortly after recording had been completed.

Ringo The 4th (Ringo only started counting with *Ringo*), released the following year,

was in any case even worse. Mardin was again the producer, and a truly impressive line-up of expert musicians had been assembled but to little effect, since the material was again very average; the majority of the tracks were composed by Ringo and his close friend, Vini Poncia.

The response to *Ringo The 4th* was generally an embarrassed one, and sales were accordingly low. Atlantic quickly cancelled his contract (though the Polydor arrangement stayed intact for the time being). Ringo moved on to CBS's Portrait label, for whom he recorded *Bad Boy*, an album that was released with some haste to coincide with a television special. Paul's experience five years earlier had not deterred Ringo from signing up for his own hour-long TV programme, but rock stars and commercial television seem temperamentally unsuited to one another, and the result (some would say, the wholly predictable result) was another cast-iron flop; *Rolling Stone* remarked simply that the programme was "disastrous".

Bad Boy was also a failure. Now that Ringo had severed his links with Atlantic, Vini Poncia had produced the album for him, but the result was still a selection of amorphous music that lacked distinguishing features. "*Bad Boy* isn't even passable cocktail music," wrote *Rolling Stone's* reviewer. "Ringo isn't even very likeable any more, and that truly is depressing." Certainly, his recording career had ground to a halt; he had become absorbed into the West Coast coterie of famous names and, like some of them, was turning out albums that were perfectly played and perfectly characterless. Like John and George before him, Ringo decided that a break from recording might prove advantageous.

His career activities subsequently became more sporadic, although this can partly be explained by the fact that he became seriously ill in Monte Carlo, where he was then living, in March 1979, and was rushed to hospital, suffering from long-term effects of his childhood illness of peritonitis.

At the beginning of 1980 he returned to the movies, a direction he might have exploited more profitably in previous years, to make *Caveman*, a film described as a zany pre-historic Western. Filming took place in Mexico in February and March 1980 and, although the screenplay eschewed the use of contemporary language, preferring to invent

Ringo became seriously ill in Monte Carlo, where he was then living, and in 1980 he returned to the movies to make 'Caveman'.

April, 1981 –
Ringo brings the Beatles together again

a primitive tongue for the occasion, Ringo managed to communicate successfully with his co-star Barbara Bach (whose previous films included *The Spy Who Loved Me* and *Force 10 From Navarone*) and a relationship between them developed swiftly towards the end of filming. Ringo's marriage to Maureen was by now dissolved, and he and Barbara were soon making plans to get married – plans that were fortunately not interrupted when the couple were involved in what might have been a serious accident in Ringo's Mercedes in South London on May 19, 1980. Luckily, they both escaped with scratches. They finally did get married almost a year later (Barbara's first marriage had been to an Italian businessman, and so divorce proceed-

ings had inevitably been lengthy) on April 27, 1981, at Marylebone register office. Once again, it was Ringo who brought the Beatles together, and the next morning's papers were full of pictures of Ringo, Paul and George all together.

Ringo felt that the car accident had been a significant moment in the relationship, and planned to display the wreckage as a piece of sculpture in their new home. He also ordered two star-shaped gold pins for Barbara and himself. "Each one has a little piece of broken windscreen set in its centre," Barbara explained to *Playboy*. "Richard" – she preferred his real name to Ringo – "felt that if we survived *that* together, we'll manage to get through a whole lot more."

Paul, and George and Olivia arrive for Ringo's wedding to American actress, Barbara Bach. The three surviving Beatles are now married to American women.

1975/'76 the Wings world tour – a more exacting schedule than anything the Beatles attempted

With the success of *Band On The Run* and *Venus And Mars*, Paul had established himself individually, and Wings' world tour from 1975-6 enabled him to establish the band as well. The U.S. leg took place in spring, and climaxed with performances at Madison Square Garden on May 24 and 25. European dates included a show in St Marks Square, Venice, on September 26, a UNESCO benefit to aid the preservation of that city's sinking treasures. The tour had included sixty-six concerts in eleven countries, and was finally brought to a conclusion in October, back home in London, with concerts at the Empire Pool, Wembley.

Apart from Harrison's brief and unhappy 1974 U.S. tour, no ex-Beatle had previously undertaken such extensive touring commitments, which, after all, were far more musically demanding than any dates the Beatles had ever done. One might understand Paul's determination to hang fire until he knew that the band was quite ready for such an arduous programme, and he had chosen his moment well. Every concert was a sell-out. By now he had virtually two audiences – the '60s Beatles one, and the one that Wings had created for itself. The tour was a huge success, and received laudatory notices at every port of call, and rapturous audience responses everywhere – in America particularly at those points in the programme where Paul chose to perform Beatles' songs, 'Lady Madonna', 'I've Just Seen A Face' or 'Yesterday', for example; but Paul was happy to include such material, since he no longer felt the Beatles' legend suffocating his career. He had led Wings from being a fledgling unit with about four songs in its repertoire, touring Britain by van and playing unpublicised college shows, to become one of the world's top rock attractions in its own right.

George Harrison had filmed and recorded the dates on his tour, but the negative response to it meant that both tapes and film were left on the shelf. Paul similarly liked to record and film everything. By this time, the costs of financing live shows had become so astronomical that rock tours usually lost money, and were only made viable by the increased album sales that they stimulated. This is certain to have been the case with Wings' shows, which possessed their fair share of spectacle – lasers, dry ice, et cetera. So that even though money would have been no object for him, it nevertheless made sense for Paul to recoup what he could through ancillary undertakings like records and films. He therefore resolved to make use of both tapes and film, assignments which were to prove curiously protracted.

There was little problem with the live album of the tour, *Wings Over America*, which was in the shops in time for Christmas. It was constructed as a complete stage performance, from opening number to final encore. Although inevitably expensive, it was nevertheless reckoned to be of high quality. It is exciting, atmospheric, and features a splendid range of material.

Wings Over America was similarly the title of a television special, shown in the U.S. on March 16, 1979, which followed the band on tour across the country, and included snippets of several concert performances. The tour also spawned a full-length feature film, *Rockshow*, which astonishingly did not have its premiere until it opened in London in March 1981. How it had taken five years to prepare, McCartney, a supposed workaholic, was at a loss to explain.

As it happened, the film was simply a straightforward souvenir of one entire show, in Seattle. For all the apparent simplicity of the concept, this was something that no rock band had previously attempted (perhaps because there was never just one show that was of high enough standard from start to finish). It was a new departure in rock movies; there was literally no extraneous camera-work – no backstage shots, or anything.

Although its dilatory arrival meant that the film had no enormous commercial impact, it was nevertheless enjoyable and successful, and it's interesting to examine the reasons why. First of all, McCartney has to choose to perform from his repertoire those songs that are already the most finished, and then he has to score them for the band (and the four-man horn section which Wings used), and sometimes extend them, making them more satisfyingly complete. In other words, his most notoriously wayward characteristics as a recording artist – his lack of concentration, his musical doodlings, his tendency not to draw compositions to a natural and disciplined conclusion – are automatically expunged simply by the mechanics necessary in putting together a stage performance. Had McCartney recorded about a third as much, but toured about three times as often, his post-Beatle career would have burgeoned in all possible ways.

As it was, his recording career did indeed lapse back into familiar pitfalls during the second half of the '70s. *Wings At The Speed Of Sound* had been released in April 1976, just before the commencement of the band's touring schedule. It was the album with which McCartney made concrete his oft-repeated assertions that Wings was a group, and not just him, since all members of the band were awarded an individual lead vocal (Paul had kindly written something called 'Cook Of The House' specially for Linda to sing), and both McCulloch and Laine had a solo composition on the album.

Inevitably, though, the most important contributions were Paul's own. A track called 'Silly Love Songs' was indicative of the state of the art as far as he was concerned. *"Some people want to fill the world with silly love songs,"* sang Paul, adding, *"And what's wrong with that?"* It was almost a treatise, informing the public that satisfying the market requirements of the time, whatever some critics might feel about it, was something that he enjoyed doing, and furthermore did rather well. Perfectly, actually. And if tossing off multi-million sellers is that easy, why doesn't everyone else do it?

The suggestions that he should aim for more significance in his work were hammered home relentlessly and if they niggled him, they did no more than that. From 'Silly Love Songs' he felt able to scorn them, and only re-examined his objectives when commercial acceptance dried up.

Wings At The Speed Of Sound, with McCartney and Wings promoting it in person through the U.S. tour, enjoyed great commercial success, and both that and the first single, 'Silly Love Songs' inevitably, topped their respective charts in the U.S. The second single from the album, 'Let 'Em In', a song in honour of family life, also reached No. 1 in the U.S. This was the album's finest track and, as *Rockshow* would demonstrate five years later, was a very effective stage number.

Though *Speed Of Sound* had been an exception, McCartney had lately been in-augurating a tradition of recording Wings' albums in exotic locations (*Band On The Run* had been made in Nigeria, and *Venus And Mars* in New Orleans). When the band assembled to record their next album in February 1977, London really seemed too deadly, and too wet. So McCartney chartered three yachts in the Caribbean, and much of *London Town* was, inappropriately enough,

recorded while the band were cruising amongst the Virgin Islands.

In fact, the album took a whole year to complete, and wasn't ready for release until April 1978. There was, therefore, a gap of two years between albums of wholly new material, a gap which Paul decided to bridge by issuing a new single. He had two songs completed, the rock number 'Girls' School' and 'Mull Of Kintyre', a song of homage to his Scottish retreat, recorded on site with the Campbell-town Pipe Band. Of the two, 'Girls' School' was clearly the more commercial.

"I had a long discussion with McCartney about 'Mull Of Kintyre'," recalled Bob Mercer. "He didn't think it would sell a copy. I thought he was off his head, and he took an awful lot of convincing that the song had some commercial potential. In fact, I never did succeed in convincing him, which is why the single was released as a double-A side, and why 'Girls' School' was made the A-side in the U.S.

"Now, when he made 'Goodnight Tonight' the following year, he sent a test pressing to me because apparently there'd been considerable discussion among his own associates about whether or not the song would be a hit, since it was unusual for McCartney to do anything that disco-slanted. I'd learned by this time that there was no point in being dishonest with him, because he was just going to do what he wanted anyway. So, I listened to it, and told him I didn't think it was very good, or that it would be a hit. So then I got a call saying, would I listen to the B-side, 'Daytime Nighttime Suffering', and I thought that was worse. So, 'Goodnight Tonight' was made the A-side, and in fact, it did very well, it reached No. 5 in the charts.

"Now, I have seen Paul frequently refer in interviews to the fact that the guy at the record company had told him that the song wouldn't be a hit, and this was Paul's way of demonstrating that you shouldn't listen to record company advice.

Had McCartney recorded about a third as much, but toured about three times as often, his post-Beatle career would have burgeoned in all possible ways. But 'Goodnight Tonight' restored Paul to chart favour. Below: 'Mull of Kintyre' has become as seasonal as Christmas pudding in the UK.

"I haven't seen him refer anywhere to the fact that it was his considered opinion that 'Mull Of Kintyre' would be lucky to sell a copy."

'Mull Of Kintyre' was the kind of family favourite that is as seasonal as Christmas pudding in the U.K. It was released in the second week of November, and by January it had sold over two million copies, making it the top-selling single of all time, and relegating 'She Loves You' and 'I Want To Hold Your Hand' respectively to second and third place. To date, 'Mull Of Kintyre' has sold over two-and-a-half million copies in the U.K. It was a hit virtually throughout the world, except, strangely enough in the U.S., where it did poorly. Whether or not this was because the song was originally released as the B-side, and only subsequently promoted as the A-side, one can only speculate.

'Mull Of Kintyre' thus became yet another astonishing triumph for McCartney; but just as his early solo career had been developed in the impossible shadow of the Beatles' success, so now 'Mull Of Kintyre' overwhelmed his efforts during the next couple of years.

By the time London Town was released, both McCulloch and English had left Wings, which was therefore reduced to the same depleted state as at the time of the release of Band On The Run. However, history didn't repeat itself, and London Town was generally considered the weakest Wings' album since Wild Life.

On Speed Of Sound, Paul had successfully adopted a 'soft' approach, and there was similarly an absence of hard rock numbers on London Town. Few tracks were very convincing, and the album as a whole seemed lightweight and unimaginative. (Several songs were written in collaboration with Denny Laine, and 'Mull Of Kintyre' had also been jointly credited to them, but the songwriting partnership was not resumed after

this.) 'With A Little Luck', the track chosen as a single, did reach No. 5 in the U.K., but two other singles subsequently released ('I've Had Enough' and the title-track) were, by McCartney standards, not successes.

Although 'Goodnight Tonight', released early in 1979, restored him to chart favour, Paul clearly felt that he needed to recover a more abrasive style for his next album, to step more closely in line with contemporary music, and to return to rock. This change of emphasis is indicated most obviously by the album's title, Back To The Egg. It is also noticeable that Paul took on board a co-producer for the first time in his solo career. The man chosen for the job was Chris Thomas, an appropriate choice because he was intimately associated with new wave music through his productions for the Sex Pistols and the Pretenders, and also because he had, many years earlier, been an assistant to George Martin during work on the White Album. Further, Paul had in the past conceived his albums in splendid isolation – i.e. with or without his group, but only exceptionally with outside assistance. This was in complete contrast to George and Ringo who had always worked with a quota of top business names, and even John, who had shown considerably less enthusiasm for working with celebrated session-players, had occasionally been joined by star names such as Elton John on recording sessions. This time, Paul not only enlisted the assistance of erstwhile Apple recording artistes, the Black Dyke Mills Band, but he also invited a host of rock stars to play on a couple of tracks, and become part of an ad hoc unit christened Rockestra. Among those who found their way to Lympne Castle, Kent, the singular location chosen for this album, were: Pete Townshend and Kenney Jones of the Who;

Dave Gilmour (Pink Floyd); John Paul Jones and the late John Bonham (Led Zeppelin); Hank Marvin (The Shadows), Ronnie Lane, and Gary Brooker.

Wings had been brought back to full strength for the album, with the addition of two relative unknowns, Steve Holly (drums) and Laurence Juber (guitar), and the entire group posed on the well-conceived cover – easily the album's strongest point. Though side one closed strongly with a rocker, 'Old Siam, Sir' and the melodic 'Arrow Through Me', the music itself failed to come up to scratch. Sometimes, the tracks were punctuated by extraneous sounds – radio noises, for example; on side two there were brief readings – from the owner of Lympne Castle – from *The Sport Of Kings* by Ian Hay and John Galsworthy's *The Little Man*. But if an overall concept had been intended, it was a pretty half-baked one.

Rolling Stone was particularly cruel about the album. "It is just about the sorriest grab

Paul's backing band on 'Coming Up' –
The Plastic Macs.

Paul McCartney – the most successful composer and recording artist, and the holder of the largest number of gold discs

bag of dreck in recent memory," claimed the reviewer, mercilessly. "*Back To The Egg* doesn't contain one cut that's the least bit fleshed out or brought to any logical conclusion." It was the familiar McCartney problem. He had every essential creative requirement, except the discipline required to knead the parts into a perfect whole. The album was particularly weak lyrically – most of the words seemed to exist in a vacuum. No less an authority than John Lennon tried to pin down the problem: "Paul is quite a capable lyricist who doesn't think he is. 'Hey, Jude' is a damn good set of lyrics. I made no contribution there. And a couple of lines he has come up with show indications of a good lyricist. But he hasn't taken it anywhere." (*Playboy*, January 1981.)

Back To The Egg sold poorly, failed to yield any hit singles ('Old Siam, Sir' reached No. 35 in the U.K.) and overstocked stores were selling it at a heavily discounted price within months of its release. It was another case of McCartney changing direction and making concessions to his audience, and coming a cropper in the process.

McCartney must have been very disappointed, since he does appear to have tried hard with the album – the time taken over the preparation of the cover was indicative enough of that. (The previous album, *London Town* had had an especially shoddy cover.) Such disappointments were soon forgotten.

At the end of October, the *Guinness Book Of Records* presented McCartney with a rhodium disc (the metal was estimated to be twice as valuable as platinum) to commemorate his achievement in becoming the most successful composer of all time, the holder of the largest number of gold discs and, simply, the world's most successful recording artist.

The exact veracity of the statistics could

perhaps be disputed (and the presentation, after all, had been concocted merely to give a well-publicised send-off to the latest edition of the *Guinness B Of R*), but the central claim was unassailable: despite a somewhat erratic performance, McCartney had created a success record in the '70s to match even that of the '60s, and no one could equal that. Further he had done it at a cost of far less personal wear and tear. Health, home, family and sanity had all been scrupulously preserved.

During November and December the new Wings formation took to the road for the first time, playing a series of U.K. gigs that commenced in Liverpool, as a form of triumphal homecoming for McCartney. There were four concerts at the Royal Court theatre, and special shows for both a family gathering ("There's quite a few of the McCartney clan about; they all breed like rabbits," explained Paul) and present-day pupils of his old school.

Just after Christmas, Wings arrived at Hammersmith Odeon for the closing night of the Concerts for Kampuchea, a series of charity shows that McCartney himself had been instrumental in instigating. He had received an invitation from Kurt Waldheim, U.N. Secretary-General, to do what he could for the plight of South-East Asians – a Beatles reunion, perchance?

Even for the U.N., that particular matter was still a no-go area, but McCartney wanted to do something. There would be no Beatles, he told Waldheim, but Wings were prepared to fill the bill (or, rather, to top it).

Nonetheless, the December 29 concert was anticipated with all the customary 'Beatles to re-form?' press hysteria (and, to be truthful, McCartney himself had helped to fan the flames: "there is always the chance", he told John Blake of the *Evening News* on November 30). As it happened, Paul did re-create a star-studded Rockestra for the occasion: Pete Townshend, Kenney Jones, John Bonham, John Paul Jones, Robert Plant, Ronnie Lane and Gary Brooker were all present, though John, George and Ringo were not.

The possibility of two million people starving in Kampuchea had aroused a fantastic emotional response in the West, and it is not surprising that McCartney should have been concerned. Even so, it was unusual for him to lend his name to the cause. Because of their fund-raising potential, the Beatles throughout their careers must have been the objects of constant interest by charity organisations. Usually, they had tried hard not to involve themselves in such matters, feeling a scepticism articulated by Lennon in his *Playboy* interview: "I don't want to have anything to do with benefits. I have been benefited to death. They're always rip-offs. The show is always a mess and the artist always comes off badly." On the whole, Paul concurred with such sentiments. "Any charity thing is dodgy," he told *Rolling Stone* (February 21, 1980), "but hopefully there's enough attention on this one to make sure it actually gets there. If you can't trust UNICEF, who can you trust?"

As it turned out, the whole enterprise did become problematical, though there is no evident blame to be attached to UNICEF. Because the Hammersmith Odeon is a relatively small venue, with limited potential in box-office takings, it had always been anticipated that the majority of the fund raised would accrue from the ancillary projects – a film and album of the event. However, both of these encountered extraordinary delays, largely because of the number of artists who'd been associated with the event throughout its four-day duration. There were a vast number of managers, agents, lawyers, financial advisers, record companies, *et al* who needed to be consulted in order to ensure that everyone was contractually entitled to appear. The record business seemed to have established a formidable bureaucracy all of its own. The television film was not screened until January 1981, and the double-album was not released until April 1981, by which time aid teams had begun withdrawing from Kampuchea as the battle against the immediate threat of mass starvation had long been won.

Obviously, McCartney was not in any way responsible for the many difficulties surrounding the film and album, but the whole episode would nevertheless have provided him with further proof of the sad but inescapable fact that charity gigs are bad news for rock stars.

After the Kampuchea concerts in January 1980, Wings flew to Tokyo for what should have been McCartney's first Japanese concerts since the Beatles' final world tour of 1966. He didn't, however, get to see much of the country or its people. He was arrested at Narita airport for possession of marijuana.

It was his first drugs charge since 1972, and the practically overt manner in which he was carrying it (in a plastic bag prominently positioned inside his suitcase) suggests that he had simply lost all fear of discovery. That it was a major *faux pas* quickly became clear. Japanese drug laws are particularly harsh, and he could have faced up to seven years in prison. Not surprisingly, worldwide interest in the affair was intense. McCartney was back on all the front pages.

At length, the Japanese authorities prudently decided to spare themselves the antipathy they would undoubtedly have generated by incarcerating the world's most successful recording artist. They accordingly deemed ten days' anxious detention, together with the complete cancellation of his scheduled tour

January, 1980, Paul arrested at Narita airport for possession of marijuana

(for which all parties were personally reimbursed by McCartney) to be sufficient punishment, and he was deported from the country on January 26.

He recovered from the experience in characteristic style, by setting himself to work. He recorded a new solo album, *McCartney II,* in a Sussex farmhouse near his home in Rye. When it was released, it went straight to No. 1, a by-now surprising occurrence (the album, after all, followed the failure of *Back To The Egg*), which was presumably explained by the renewed interest in McCartney's career after the vast publicity his Tokyo experiences had aroused. It also helped, of course, that the album included a hit single, 'Coming Up', which scorched up the charts. (In the U.S. a different, live version of the song proved to be the hit. It had been recorded in Glasgow, on the last night of Wings' U.K. tour.)

In fact, *McCartney II* proved to be little more than a tale of two ditties, because apart from 'Coming Up' and a second hit single, 'Waterfalls', it had little to recommend it. Lyrically, it was wholly inadequate. "McCartney hits a new low – again," affirmed *Rolling Stone.*

Reactions such as these no doubt induced further doubts in Paul about his own creative abilities, and he looked for guidance in the one direction he might have looked all along. He asked George Martin to produce his next album. All those still concerned for the welfare of McCartney's career must have rejoiced at this news. After all, McCartney and Martin had worked together only once since the Beatles' bust-up (on the soundtrack of *Live And Let Die*); one has only to go back to *Abbey Road* to appreciate the potency of the combination in its day, and to realise that McCartney's creativity was clearly in far better shape when Martin was helping to channel it.

Once the approach had been made, and Martin had accepted the commission McCartney seems to have worked with refreshed zeal, writing material throughout the autumn, and recording during the winter at Martin's AIR studios on Montserrat in the West Indies.

Wings had disintegrated by this time. Holly and Juber had both gone their separate ways during 1980, and the faithful Laine at last departed in April 1981, leaving on the brink of what would have been his tenth anniversary with the band.

While McCartney's career as a professional musician was subject to occasional vicissitudes, he had no such problems with his business affairs. Indeed, his determination to leave his affairs in the hands of the Eastmans at the time when the other three preferred Klein's services was vindicated over and over again during the '70s. When Lee Eastman, seeking guidance in ways of investing Paul's money, had inquired what he was interested in, the latter replied, "Music." He said he especially liked Buddy Holly, and so they purchased on his behalf the publishing rights to the Holly catalogue. Paul, not wishing simply to increase the yield of this new source of income, but rather to perpetuate the name of his heroes, accordingly arranged Buddy Holly weeks in early September, to coincide with the anniversary of Holly's birth. Special guest at the inaugural one in 1976 was Norman Petty, Holly's producer, and the weeks soon became an annual event. The 1978 festivities were marked by the premiere of *The Buddy Holly Story,* starring Gary Busey – and it was after attending a party to celebrate this that, sadly, Keith Moon died.

Once the acquisition of the Holly catalogue had reaped satisfying dividends (Denny Laine also recorded a complete album of Holly material, *Holly Days,* which McCart-

ney produced for him), the Eastmans displayed considerable acumen in buying up music publishing catalogues, so that McCartney was soon the owner of a host of lucrative commercial properties, including *Grease* and *Annie*.

There was also success on one other front. Linda McCartney had extended her photographic interests by working on short cartoon films, and in 1978 one of these, *The Oriental Nightfish*, animated by Ian Emes, became the official British short at the Cannes Film Festival. Another of her films, *Seaside Woman*, animated by Oscar Grillo, was chosen in 1980, and this won the *Palme d'Or*, the major prize.

"We have basically decided, without a great decision," John Lennon told a Tokyo press conference in October 1977, "to be with our baby as much as we can until we feel we can take time off to indulge ourselves in creating things outside the family."

This was one of the first, and only, public announcements that Lennon made to explain his position during the years from 1975–80, when, to the ever-increasing frustration of a public desperate for a word from their mainman, he simply did nothing – in a professional capacity, that is. He was actually quite busy.

Even within the industry, there were very few who were privy to his personal decision. "In 1975, I was with him at really important times for him personally," said Bob Mercer. "I was there at the beginning of the year because I was the person earmarked to start to talk to him about a new contract. We'd done a deal with Paul, and John's attitude was, I want the same deal as Paul. So we'd talked to his lawyers. When I told John at one stage that it looked as though we were getting close, he said, "Oh, really?" and the next day rang up to say he'd sacked his lawyers. He did that twice. Basically, he'd had enough of deals and contracts.

McCartney purchases the publishing rights to the Buddy Holly catalogue. After attending the celebration party for the premiere of 'The Buddy Holly Story', pictured here, Keith Moon died.

"We have decided," said John, "to be with our baby as much as we can until we feel we can take time off to indulge ourselves in creating things outside the family . . . I missed the first one, Julian, and I'm not going to miss this one."

"So I was there in New York, and John and Yoko were very happy, and announced that that morning Yoko had had her pregnancy confirmed. At the time, I was in the middle of talking to John about a new deal, and John said he was not going to work while Yoko was pregnant, because of her miscarriages. He was going to look after her.

"So the man's telling you that he's not going to work because he doesn't want his wife to abort – you can't look him in the eye and say, 'Well, it's more important for you to finish a new album and do a deal with EMI.' Apart from which he had been very honest and said that the last thing he was interested in doing was signing a record deal.

"What he was really saying was that prior to knowing about the pregnancy he wasn't very interested in doing deals, but he was interested in making music. After the pregnancy, he wasn't interested in making deals or making music.

"The next time I saw him happened to be straight after Yoko had come out of hospital with the baby, Sean.

"And his message was, 'I'm not going to be working for five years. I'm going to look after the baby. I missed the first one, Julian, and I'm not going to miss this one.' And again, it's very difficult to look someone in the eye and say, 'You can't do that, your career's more important.' Especially if that someone's John Lennon."

Although Mercer was certain that Lennon wouldn't work at all during those five years, he couldn't be certain that he would resume work after that passage of time. It was never really public knowledge, however, that Lennon had effectively embargoed his own career plans for that period. Consequently, the world grew fascinated, wondering what Lennon could possibly be doing and why he was apparently behaving, as Lennon himself

more than once commented, like Howard Hughes or Greta Garbo.

He did make one public appearance on July 27 1976, when his application to remain in the U.S. as a permanent resident was formally approved. Lennon, who had dressed soberly in collar and tie, and had his hair cut, for the occasion, was finally given his long-cherished Green Card, which meant that at last he could now travel in and out of the U.S. as he wished.

Henceforward, he communicated with his public largely by rumour. Solid information seemed limited to several photographs in the press of him and Yoko spending the next New Year in the company of James Taylor and Carly Simon, and three weeks later both John and Yoko attended President Carter's inaugural gala.

The rest was largely silence. It was variously reported that he'd become a house-husband, staying at home, minding the baby and

baking bread (true) and that he'd claimed to have ceased all professional activities because he'd already made his contribution to civilisation (false). From the interviews Lennon gave at the time of the release of *Double Fantasy*, when he broke his long silence, it was clear that he'd been handling the rigours of domestic life, while Yoko had been minding the store.

She handled the job with consummate skill, and swelled the family fortunes, generally by making astute investments in real estate. In addition to the seven apartments at the Dakota that they already owned, the couple purchased several properties throughout the U.S. For example, in February 1978 they

bought 1000 acres of farmland in upstate New York, where they raised Holstein cows; one of which Yoko sold at a fair in Syracuse for a record price of $265,000.

With Yoko wheeling and dealing in property circles, John would often slip away to distant parts of the world with Sean, or simply go into the Record Plant studios in New York to make recordings for just Yoko to hear.

On one occasion they breached their wall of silence themselves. In May 1979 they took a full-page ad in certain newspapers (shades of the John and Yoko of ten years earlier) to reply to all the entreaties they had received to come out of hibernation, and to explain that they were not doing so because it was time for

In August, 1980, John returned to work so that he could have 'Double Fantasy' out for Sean's fifth birthday.

"the spring cleaning of our minds". Most people found the message hopelessly dis-illusioning. John and Yoko still seemed gaga on the old '60s philosophies, an impression all but confirmed by the closing comment that "three angels were looking over our shoulders when we wrote this". There were those who still entertained hopes of a come-back, but there were many more who re-luctantly concluded that Lennon was not interested in resuming recording activities, but that even if he were the results would be unsatisfactory; with little more than wild rumours and the three angels message on which to base to their assumptions, many were resigned to the fact that Lennon seemed a spent force. He was behaving just like an eccentric millionaire in premature dotage.

That this impression should have been quite as widespread as it was is presumably a testament to the success with which he had buried himself for the public gaze. For throughout it all he had remained the same as ever – witty, alert and intelligent – so that it now seems absurd that anyone could ever have doubted it.

As it happened, he didn't quite wait five years. He returned to work in August 1980 so that he could have a new album released to coincide with Sean's fifth birthday.

John was still reluctant to sign pieces of paper, but Yoko took care of all the business aspects, and in the end they both signed to David Geffen's newly-formed Geffen Records. *Double Fantasy*, credited equally to John Lennon and Yoko Ono, since they took alternate tracks, was released towards the beginning of November.

Many critics were underwhelmed; they found it, after all this time, low-key and un-adventurous. Most were prepared to admit, though, that Yoko's songs, far less impenet-rable than previously, were the best she'd ever written. (In the wake of the emergence of the U.K. new wave, her style actually seemed more contemporary than John's.)

However, *Double Fantasy* was not an album that yielded all its magic on initial hearings. In many respects, the songs Lennon had written were the ones he should have composed after the release of the *Plastic Ono Band* album, for they show him emotionally purged and at peace with himself. What makes the songs so warm is that, as ever, he is being perfectly honest about his feelings. The tracks which open each side – the Roy Orbison/Elvis Presley throwback '(Just Like) Starting Over' and 'Watching The Wheels' are both strong songs, although many may have found the latter a rather superficial attempt to rationalise his five-year absence. All his other songs have their particular merits; 'Woman' is just perfect, and 'Beautiful Boy' is a lullaby which it is impossible to listen to without a sense of aching sorrow.

The point is that the particular qualities of the album soon became irrelevant.

What mattered more than that was that John Lennon was back and, as the various promotional interviews given at the time of the album's release demonstrated (the best being the *Playboy* one, and the BBC one given to Andy Peebles), he was not mentally incapacitated after all, but as bright as ever. It was the interviews, as well as the music on *Double Fantasy*, that held the promise of great things to come in the future.

What mattered then was that this renais-sance was all too quickly terminated, when he was brutally gunned down outside his Dakota apartments, returning home after more recording sessions. December 8 1980 was a day of extreme sadness for millions; entire generations felt a grievous sense of loss. There are few public figures whose death would have been mourned more.

Julian arrives at the Dakota Apartments following his father's murder

CHAPTER
8

A High Price For Success

News of the death was followed firstly by a worldwide eruption of public mourning, and secondly by tidal waves of exploitation merchandise. Beatle ephemera returned overnight to shop counters, and 'tribute' books and magazines apeared out of nowhere.

At the last, there was considerable public sympathy for Yoko Ono, who behaved with dignity and reserve after the murder. She proclaimed a round-the-world silent vigil for 2 p.m. New York time (7 p.m. in London and Liverpool) the following Sunday – a sensible idea, since it was tantamount to allowing millions of fans an opportunity to participate in the funeral. In fact, Lennon's body had been privately cremated soon after his death.

In characteristic style, Yoko took out a full-page advertisement in many Sunday newspapers in the middle of January, a letter of gratitude for the many condolences and expressions of sympathy ("I thank you for your letters, telegrams and thoughts").

Within weeks of John's death, Yoko had resumed work, recording an album of her own, *Season Of Glass*. This was released in June 1981, and boldly included references to the murder: one track, 'No, No, No' was preceded by a series of gun-shots, and the front cover grimly showed Lennon's blood-splattered spectacles. There was no direct dedication, however, for, as Yoko explained, "Many amazing things happened during the recording session. All I can say is that John was right there with me, busy trying to arrange things for me. That is why this album is not dedicated to him. He would have been offended. He was one of us."

The John-Yoko relationship was clearly a very jealous one, but it's nonsense to attribute this to one party more than the other. Yoko does seem to have been both extraordinarily self-possessed, and also extremely vulnerable. She was also very possessive, a characteristic which manifested itself in her extreme reluctance that John should re-visit Britain. But John Lennon was not only a wonderful human being, he was also a powerfully individual one, and it's absurd to imagine anyone or anything suppressing him. The

The Beatles Apart

John and Yoko relationship was their relationship, and however they managed it, that was how they wanted it. One can only regret the temerity and lack of understanding of the girls in the audiences at Beatles conventions in the late '70s who would boo and hiss whenever Yoko or Linda were mentioned, or appeared on film. "Yoko's taken a lot of shit," Ringo told *Rolling Stone*, "her and Linda; but the Beatles' break-up wasn't their fault. It was just that suddenly we were all thirty and married and changed. We couldn't carry on that life any more." On one level, it's amazing that Yoko and Linda should still be cast as the villains of the piece; on another, it's a characteristic of the Beatles' story as a whole that the women who feature in it have always been under-estimated.

Ringo was the only one of the Beatles to fly to console Yoko in person after John's death. One can assume that Paul, just about to begin a recording stint in Montserrat, and George, likewise recording busily at the studio in his Henley home, were both stunned. The effect of the murder was naturally to increase the concerns of each for his own safety. Ringo, the only one living outside the U.K., has a 24-hour security guard at his Los Angeles home, though he will probably now return to live in Britain.

It was in any case unfortunate that Ringo, with homes in Los Angeles, Monte Carlo and London, should have been in tax exile at all, because he had a very strong family unit at home. All four always had well-grounded family roots back in Liverpool, and surely that was one of the factors which kept them level-headed and relatively sane throughout it all.

The '70s in fact were a particularly tragic time for Ringo, because he lost three of his closest friends in just over three years – Marc Bolan, Keith Moon and John Lennon. He had also become acquainted with Mae West, just before she died, after taking a cameo role in her last film, *Sextette*.

In other ways, Ringo seemed the odd one out. The other three all managed to use their money to make further fortunes in something outside their immediate career – Paul in song-publishing, George in film production with *Life Of Brian*, and John in real estate. Ringo, the lonesome drummer left without a gig, didn't seem to have anything left, apart from a stuttering film career.

All four had their artistic troughs during the '70s, when they seemed to have lost the knack of making good music: Paul with *Ram* and *Wild Life*, John (*Some Time In New York City* and *Mind Games*), George (*Dark Horse* and *Extra Texture*) and Ringo (*Ringo The Fourth* and *Bad Boy*). Thus Ringo is the only one, as yet, not to have recovered from such difficulties. Nevertheless, all three, surviving Beatles were working actively in the wake of Lennon's death, and all had albums slated for release in summer 1981. Ringo's, *Can't Fight Lightning*, included material by both Paul and George; John had delivered songs to him on November 15, the last time he saw him, which he had decided not to use for the moment.

It always seemed that one of the greatest mistakes the individual Beatles made was to cast aside so peremptorily George Martin, since they felt he was receiving more than his fair share of credit for Beatles' recordings. Most Beatle fans, while hardly denying that the music itself came from the band, would acknowledge that his influence was vital. When the four were together as the Beatles their creativity had two filters – first of all, each other, and, secondly, Martin. That they should lose both simultaneously made it inevitable that their music might occasionally become self-indulgent and undisciplined –

something which happened to all four at one stage or another. Perhaps in many ways it's highly creditable that each accomplished as much as he did during the '70s.

The Lennon murder was nevertheless an awful conclusion to a period in which, up until then, they had successfully retreated from the mayhem of Beatlemania, and overcome the enormous psychological and artistic problems that were part of its legacy.

The public '60s had become the private '70s, and it seemed miraculous that they had survived everything, and emerged healthy, happy and domestically secure. Lennon's death smashed the illusion that personalities as public as the Beatles once were can ever hope to win ultimate security and privacy as individuals. They already paid a high price for their success, and sadly it seems as though they are expected to go on paying.

Discography

George Harrison
Wonderwall Music (Apple 1968)
Electronic Sounds (Zapple 1969)
All Things Must Pass (Apple 1970)
Living In The Material World (Apple 1973)
Dark Horse (Apple 1974)
Extra Texture (Apple 1975)
Thirty Three & ⅓ (Dark Horse 1976)
The Best Of George Harrison (Parlophone 1977)
George Harrison (Dark Horse 1979)
Somewhere In England (Dark Horse 1981)

Contributions to:
The Concert for Bangla Desh (Apple 1972)

John Lennon
Unfinished Music No. 1 – Two Virgins (Apple 1968)
Unfinished Music No. 2 – Life With The Lions (Zapple 1969)
The Wedding Album (Apple 1969)
Plastic Ono Band/Live Peace In Toronto (Apple 1969)
John Lennon/Plastic Ono Band (Apple 1970)
Imagine (Apple 1971)
Some Time In New York City (Apple 1972)
Mind Games (Apple 1973)
Walls And Bridges (Apple 1974)
Rock 'n' Roll (Apple 1975)
Shaved Fish (Collectable Lennon) (Apple 1975)
Double Fantasy (Geffen 1980)

Ringo Starr
Sentimental Journey (Apple 1970)
Beaucoups Of Blues (Apple 1970)
Ringo (Apple 1973)
Goodnight Vienna (Apple 1974)
Blast From Your Past (Apple 1975)
Ringo's Rotogravure (Polydor 1976)
Ringo The 4th (Polydor 1977)
Bad Boy (Polydor 1978)

Paul McCartney
McCartney (Apple 1970)
Ram (Apple 1971)
Wild Life (Apple 1971)
Red Rose Speedway (Apple 1973)
Band On The Run (Apple 1973)
Venus And Mars (Capitol 1975)
Wings At The Speed Of Sound (Capitol 1976)
Wings Over America (Capitol 1976)
London Town (EMI 1978)
Wings Greatest (EMI 1978)
Back To The Egg (EMI 1979)
McCartney II (Parlophone 1980)

Also:
The McCartney Interview (Parlophone 1980)

Contributions to:
Concerts For The People Of Kampuchea
  (Atlantic 1981)

Bibliography

Roy Carr and Tony Tyler *The Beatles, An Illustrated Record (revised edition)* (New English Library 1978)

Harry Castleman and Walter J. Podrazik *All Together Now* (The Pierian Press, 1976)

Ray Connolly *John Lennon 1940–1980* (Fontana 1981)

Richard DiLello *The Longest Cocktail Party* (Charisma 1973)

Anthony Fawcett *John Lennon: One Day At A Time* (New English Library 1977)

Goldie Friede, Robin Titone and Sue Weiner *The Beatles A to Z* (Eyre Methuen 1981)

Vic Garbarini and Brian Cullman with Barbara Graustark *Strawberry Fields Forever: John Lennon Remembered* (Bantam 1980)

Cynthia Lennon *A Twist Of Lennon* (Star 1978)

Nick Logan and Bob Woffinden *The Illustrated Encyclopedia Of Rock (revised edition)* (Salamander 1977)

Peter McCabe and Robert D. Schonfield *Apple To The Core* (Martin Brian & O'Keeffe 1972)

Ross Michaels *George Harrison Yesterday and Today* (Flash Books, 1977)

Miles *John Lennon In His Own Words* (Omnibus 1981)

Philip Norman *Shout! The True Story of The Beatles* (Elm Tree 1981)

Andy Peebles *The Lennon Tapes* (BBC 1981)

Nicholas Schaffner *The Beatles Forever (revised edition)* (McGraw-Hill 1978)

Derek Taylor *As Time Goes By* (Abacus 1974)

Jann Wenner *Lennon Remembers* (Penguin 1973)

Picture Credits
United Press International
Popperfoto
Syndication International
Keystone Press
Rex Features
London Features International
Camera Press

Front cover based upon 'Let It Be' (EMI).
Photographs by Ethan Russell.